Wondrous British Marine Life

A HANDBOOK FOR COASTAL EXPLORERS

Lou Luddington

To Jen,
Happy Birthday
Maybe one day we can reunite
on a coastline somewhere and
adventure together!
Cariad Mawr
With Amber
_27.4.21_

First published in Great Britain 2019 by Pesda Press

Tan y Coed Canol
Ceunant
Caernarfon
Gwynedd
LL55 4RN

ISBN: 9781906095703

Printed and bound in Poland, www.hussarbooks.pl

"Education is not the filling of a pale, but the lighting of a fire."

W.B. Yeats

Acknowledgements

From the depths of my heart I would like to thank Ron and Joey (mum and dad) for encouraging me as a young swimmer and naturalist to work hard and bring my dreams of becoming a marine biologist to fruition. Much gratitude goes to Lyndon Lomax for giving me permission to use his wonderful images of a sunfish, common dolphins, bottlenose dolphins and Risso's dolphin, Dave Boyle for his Manx shearwater image and Trevor Rees for his image of a mauve stinger. Thanks to the Pembrokeshire Coastal Forum for permission to reproduce one of the Pembrokeshire Marine Code maps. Many, many thanks go to John Hegley, whose blessing to use an excerpt from his brilliant poem *'I Am A Guillemot'* in the *Seabirds* chapter gave me happy heart flutterings; I sincerely recommend his book of poems *'I AM A POETATO'* for those days when you just need to laugh. I am indebted to my niece Jordan whose wonderful design skills transformed my scribbly drawings; I have a lasting mental image of her expertly navigating Photoshop one-handed, laptop balanced on her knees while breast feeding baby Arlo. In a final crescendo of gratitude this book is dedicated to Tom, whose unfaltering belief that I can do 'the thing' keeps me reaching for the stars.

About the Author

Dr Lou Luddington is a marine biologist and photographer with a love for spending lots of time outdoors in nature. During her formative years Lou developed a connection with water and the natural world through competitive swimming, bird watching, backyard natural history and photography. Studying marine biology at the University of Wales, Bangor was an exciting and natural progression. There she gained a degree and PhD in marine biology and spent many hours underwater honing her skills as a scientific diver. Since then she has worked in marine monitoring and conservation and in the outdoor sector as an activity and wildlife guide, becoming a PADI Dive Master, British Canoeing 4-star sea kayak leader, surf coach and certified Marine Mammal Observer along the way. Alongside nature and in-water photography commissions, Lou runs professional development courses for outdoor guides and instructors on coastal and marine life. She also writes a column for the sea kayaking magazine Ocean Paddler on marine life and is an ambassador for Palm Equipment and Rockpool kayaks. In 2018 Lou had her first photography exhibition "The Sea From Within", a

milestone and launch pad for making her images available as fine art prints www.louluddington.com. After 17 blissful years living in Solva, Pembrokeshire with magician husband Tom, they have just sold up and moved aboard their 35ft sailing yacht *Noctiluca*. They named their boat after the bioluminescent plankton that lights up the ocean on dark nights (Noctiluca means night light), as they plan to be 'a light at sea', documenting and championing the marine environment through photography, video, science, writing and magic.

Follow their adventures at www.alightatsea.com.

Being small in stature and having a hard shell make a lot of sense when living in one of the most dynamic environments on the planet. Barnacles and a tube worm on the rocky shore. This image was highly commended at the British Wildlife Photography Awards 2019.

Contents

Kelp seaweeds form an important and beautiful habitat in UK waters.

Introduction

This book is a guide to marine and coastal life typically seen while exploring and journeying along the UK coast. It is not meant as an identification guide for putting scientific names to species; there are many of those out there that do a superb and concise job already which I have referred you to in the Bibliography. However, for the species included in this book I have quoted the scientific name so that you can be sure exactly which species I am referring to. Common names may vary wildly between texts and certainly between languages, while the scientific name is universal and therefore useful to know.

The aim of this guide is to bridge the gap between this plethora of natural history identification guides, and the broad body of scientific research literature that expounds the biology of the oceans. It showcases the life stories of a wide selection of coastal inhabitants, from barnacles and jellyfish to seals and lichens, and is brought to life by full colour, professional quality images from my own collection. The juiciest facts uncovered by scientific research have been cherry-picked because I believe that by encouraging you to think about how a sea anemone poos, or to ponder the astonishing length of a barnacle's penis, this book may act as a stepping-stone to further curiosity and learning.

My sole aim is to spark awe and wonder for our coastal seas by illuminating the hidden lives of those that live there. The overall ethos of the book is to impress on you a way of enjoying the natural environment that is sensitive and respectful. Most importantly, I urge you to embrace our irrefutable connection to it; with our oceans in peril from pollution, over-fishing, acidification and accelerated warming due to global climate change. The time is now.

"In the end we will conserve only what we love; we will love only what we understand; and we will understand only what we are taught." Baba Dioum, 1968.

Puffins.

Awe and Wonder

Through my own explorations while sea kayaking, freediving, surfing, scuba diving, sailing and swimming along the coast I have had some truly memorable experiences on days where everything aligned to put me in the right place. I recount many of these moments throughout the following chapters but one in particular, from a weekend on Skomer Island, provides affirmation of the sheer awe and wonder of British marine life.

Skomer Island is a magical place. Lying a few kilometres off the Pembrokeshire coast it is home to a diverse range of wildlife, including the Skomer vole, and a haven for breeding seabirds and Atlantic grey seals. Separating it from the mainland is a narrow sound that squeezes the tide into an exhilarating race, adding to the allure. A few summers ago, on the last days of July, my friend Jonny and I guided an immersive, wildlife-focused weekend of sea kayaking to Skomer Island with a night in the island bunkhouse. Blessed with ideal weather, we enjoyed two halcyon days afloat.

Day 1

Our route for the day was planned to take advantage of tidal flow and took us on an anticlockwise circumnavigation of the island. We launched from the mainland with everything we needed for two days on the water and an overnight stay in the island bunkhouse. Conditions were truly dreamy, with very little wind or swell, and blue skies above. Afloat, our small team of four clients plus me, Jonny and my husband Tom were all smiles. Pointing the

bows of our sea kayaks west towards the island, our journey began. With only half a kilometre of the mainland coast to cover before we hit open water, we tucked in near to the rocks to enjoy the detail. Low tide and calm water meant we could get a close look at some of the marine life surrounding us. Floating in the glassy water were compass, moon and blue jellyfish accompanied by their relatives the comb jellies, that differ in their lack of stinging cells with which to capture prey. Instead they use rows of beating hair-like structures that refract the light making them sparkle and shimmer. Stuck to the rocks were thousands of barnacles that had recently put on a growth spurt. I knew this from the shed exoskeletons floating in the water like hundreds of tiny feathers, ghostly replicas of the curly legs they use for feeding.

Having lingered long enough for the tide to turn we headed south through Jack Sound on a gentle ferry glide across the ebbing tide. Despite its fearsome reputation Jack Sound had granted us a mellow passage to the south side and we cruised on passed Midland Isle and over to the south coast of Skomer Island. This part of the island is deeply cleaved by narrow inlets – Rob's Wick, Matthew's Wick, South Haven and The

Wick; so striking are these features that the islands name reflects them – Skomer derives from the Norse word Skalmey which translates as cleft or cut island. At South Haven the island appears almost cut in two, separated from North Haven opposite by a narrow isthmus only a few metres wide. These steep, secluded zawns provide ideal nursery grounds for seal pups on the beaches and cliff nesting sites for birds. Our timing was such that many seabirds had fledged, leaving only streaks of white guano where birds would have jostled together in their hundreds only a few weeks earlier. Guillemots and razorbills were absent, by now far out to sea.

Seals on the other hand were gathering, brought together by carnal urges that were rising to a crescendo of autumn births and mating. We glimpsed the odd pup tucked away on boulder beaches and gave them a wide berth. Distressing the mother by approaching too close could result in a missed feed with knock-on effects for the pup's survival. With only three weeks in which to get their fill of fat-rich milk before being left to fend for themselves – every feed is vital.

Thick-necked, feisty bull seals popped up on occasion and let us know who was boss with a hearty snort and deft slap of the water with a flipper. Top of their daily agenda was hustling females and beach patrols as they waited impatiently to mate. Intimidating floating humans was a good way to pass the time as female seals would not entertain them until their pups were weened.

As we dipped into bays and ambled along the coast, a peregrine falcon, a buzzard, a pair of piping oystercatchers and a band of noisy chough punctuated our journey. Most of the 21,000 or so Atlantic puffins that visit Skomer to breed head for the open ocean by the end of July, so we were overjoyed that for some the instinctual draw to the island was still strong. Chatting with the island warden later in the day we discovered that those still around were most likely young adults prospecting for next season's breeding sites. We saw them bobbing together in rafts, whirring by overhead and standing high above us on grassy banks.

Cruising on to South Haven we paused for a time to bob with groups of puffins. The distinctive calls of kittiwakes drifted to us from a dark cliff ahead. These pretty, rather dainty gulls form noisy colonies on high cliffs where they construct thick nests from mud, seaweed and vegetation. They would occupy nest sites until August and formed one thread of our rich island soundtrack. After a brief but thrilling ride through the Mew Stone's shallow passage we emerged to Skomer's wilder south-west quarter. Here rock flowed and soared into impressive cliffs and formations – a grand display of the island's volcanic origins. Exploring close-in we became part of it all – humans, birds, seals, rock, earth and emerald ocean. Though unspoken I could sense the shared awe from the others at reaching this place.

Pushing on west we passed under Skomer Head – an imposing cliff swathed in black and orange lichens and a benchmark for the Ballantine Scale. This biologically defined wave exposure scale assigns a particular shore a number from 1 to 8 according to the marine communities living there. Skomer Head lies at number one, the most extreme of rocky shores that experiences regular, heavy ocean conditions and inhabited by a sparse and hardy collection of animals and plants.

Spice was added to the day on the north-west stretch where tide flowed around the island against us. Effort was rewarded with some travelling surf and expansive views of Ramsey Island and the Bishops and Clerks to the north. At the Garland Stone, the island's north tip, we were joined by seals doing laps in the tide. We paused for a while to enjoy their attention then pressed on to the only place to land on the island, North Haven. Hauling our kayaks up high above the slipway, we took a blissful lunch in the sun. We then gathered what we needed for our night on the island and headed up the path. After a quick tour of the bunkhouse from the island staff we excitedly grabbed binoculars and hurried off along the island paths. Littering the way were the remains of Manx shearwaters, mostly wings and a few other bones, the rest devoured by their main predators the great and lesser black-backed gulls. Skomer Island supports the world's largest breeding colony of Manx shearwaters; with around 300,000 pairs the black-backed gulls were well supplied.

Rabbits (also food for the black-backed gulls and island buzzards) hopped lazily among the path-side vegetation that was scattered with the stripy caterpillars of Cinnabar moths. These caterpillars feast on ragwort leaves, accumulating the plant's toxins in their own flesh which makes them poisonous to would-be predators.

Like many other creatures they were enjoying a life of plenty on Skomer. A glorious summer evening of birds, butterflies and rabbits passed, until our own hunger called us back to the bunkhouse. As dusk fell Tom and Jonny headed back down to their kayaks; the popularity of a night on Skomer meant we could only book five beds for me and the four clients. Tom and Jonny would make the 2.5km crossing back to the mainland for the night then return to meet us in the morning. Though they didn't know it, encounters with toads, tide races in the dark, huge rafts of noisy shearwaters, frenzied black-backed gulls and bioluminescent plankton would set their evening alight.

The rest of us joined in with the island staff's daily bird log at 9 p.m. to register our bird sighting from the day, then waited for darkness to descend. Night of the blackest sort was required for Skomer's nocturnal wildlife spectacle. We ventured out from the bunkhouse at 10.30 p.m. but all was quiet, so we decided to head back for tea and chocolate and wait a bit. On second attempt an hour later, a din flooded to our ears as we stepped into the night. Manx shearwaters were in full swing, calling to each other through the blackness. Having spent the day fishing at sea they returned to the island in the dark to avoid attacks from hungry black-backed gulls. Though beautifully adapted for a life at sea, with long narrow wings and feet placed far back on the body for efficient swimming, they are ungainly on land and an easy target for these large predatory birds.

We hurried out along the path towards North Haven, the calls growing louder. Some calls came from overhead, others from burrows in the earth; chicks safe below ground called to parents returning with bellies full of fish. Soon birds were flapping around our heads and landing at our feet. At one-point one of our group had to duck to avoid impact from a bird careering through the night. Once on the ground they would either scurry off quickly and disappear down a hole in the ground or sit for a while looking a bit dazed before deciding which way to go. With both ground and air ringing with their peculiar calls, we were in the midst of a nocturnal bird colony in full swing. Later as I drifted off to sleep to their muffled calls, I pictured thousands of sleepy birds snoozing in earthy burrows nearby.

Day 2

The next morning as we walked back down the track to our boats and retraced our steps from last night's show, all was quiet at the path-side burrows. We felt privileged to have witnessed the exclusive shearwater performance that was reserved for overnight guests on the blackest of summer nights. For our morning entertainment we were treated to stands of puffins lining the banks of the incline down to our kayaks. As we prepared to launch Jonny arrived from the mainland full of stories from a magical evening of his own. Given the continuing favourable forecast our plan was to take the south going tide through Little Sound and make the 4km crossing to Skomer's sister island Skokholm Island. Exiting North Haven to the east, passing by Rye Rocks a seal slid into the water and started following us. Whisked through Little Sound by the tide, the seal was still with us, enjoying a free ride. Our escort provided entertainment not only for the crossing but for almost the entire circumnavigation of the island. When we stopped so did seal, reaching up to play with our bow and stern toggles and swimming belly-up beneath our kayaks then popping up to look us straight in the eyes. He was clearly having fun. When we reached the island and stopped to rest, he turned his nose skyward and howled like a wolf. It was only when we reached Hog Bay at the south-east end of the island, an hour into our new partnership that he vanished. The group of seals that greeted us and bobbed and eyed us warily, broke the bond with our Skomer seal and left us wondering at our travelling companion's fate.

On the return crossing to the mainland, a stiffening breeze provided a lumpy sea state to occupy our thoughts. At the half-way point we were treated to a sighting of mother and calf porpoise travelling with the tide. Reaching the south Marloes peninsula we tucked in close for some rock hopping and were startled when a white rock morphed into a seal pup. As we hastily backed away the mother landed beside the pup and started to suckle. This stretch of coast has many secluded coves and hidden caves popular for pupping so we were vigilant for other nursing seals.

With a quickening north going tide and a fair north-west breeze against it, Jack Sound was starting to look sporty. To reach the north coast and our landing at Martin's Haven, we would need to commit to the main flow but there was one more cave to explore before we did so. Jonny and one of the group headed in first and disappeared for several minutes. Just when the rest of us were beginning to wonder if all was well in there Jonny popped back through grinning and told us to follow on. In single file we threaded our kayaks through the narrow passage, paddles stowed, feeling our way with hands on either wall, until we slid out into the light. We had tunnelled right through Wooltack Point headland and by-passed Jack Sound. Emerging from the darkness was like waking from a dream, a symbolic return from a magical world of seal friends, burrowing seabirds and candy-striped caterpillars. We returned to the mainland with full hearts and a feeling that all was good in the world.

Bands of life colour the rocky coast in a striking example of ecological zonation.

Zonation – the Stripy Coast

Glance around the rocky coasts of the temperate northern hemisphere and you will see a black line like smudged charcoal fading off into the distance. Look a little closer and you may notice an orange band of colour above it and pale green yet higher still. If it happens to be low tide, below the black line your eye may be drawn to a buff-coloured zone and further seaward a dark brown zone that ends at the water's edge. These colours are not the rock itself but a living veneer of encrusting lichens, sedentary animals and seaweeds. Above the high-tide mark their distribution is determined by tolerance to salt spray, while between the tides a complex interaction of factors that include competition, predation, tolerance to wave action, temperature fluctuations, desiccation and food availability comes into play. Here we will take a closer look at this colourful, vertical scale of life.

1 Black tar lichen up-close appears daubed onto the rock.

2 Black tar lichen growing high up the cliff on a wave-exposed coast.

3 Black tar lichen extends less than half a metre up the rocks in the shelter of a harbour.

4 The orange lichen Xanthoria parietina thrives on rock enriched with poo.

5 The orange sea star Caloplaca thallincola grow as neat rosettes on the rock.

6 Caloplaca marina forms loose, sprawling rosettes with pale margins.

7 The greenish-grey tufts of sea ivory are very brittle when dry and wonderfully soft and pliable when wet.

8 The grey crusts of black shield lichen are strikingly dotted with the black disc-shaped fruiting bodies.

Lichens

Along the rocky coast lichens inhabit the margins of the land where conditions are too dry for marine organisms to survive and too salty for those of terrestrial origins; they form one of the classic examples of ecological zonation. Each type of lichen has adapted to living at a particular height on the shore through its own conditional preferences so that their distribution forms a colourful, vertical scale of tolerance to splash from salt-laden sea spray. The width of each distinct band varies with exposure to wind and swell, such that each becomes wider and starts higher up the rocks as the shore becomes more exposed to waves. Closest to the waterline and extending below the high-tide mark a black, crust-like layer of tar lichen thrives where rock is routinely splashed by waves and immersed at high water of spring tides. This lichen has the appearance of dried tar on the rocks, hence its name. On the west-facing cliffs of offshore islands black tar lichen may extend 30 metres or more up the cliffs, while in the calm shelter of natural harbours it spans less than a metre in height. By simply observing the vertical extent of black tar lichen on any particular shore it is possible to assess the overall liveliness of the adjacent sea.

Above the black tar lichen and preferring less spray are the orange lichens *Xanthoria parietina*, the orange sea lichen *Caloplaca marina*, and the orange sea star *Caloplaca thallincola*. *Xanthoria parietina* prefers nutrient enriched sites, often flourishing where animals routinely poo. The Inuit people of northern Alaska and Canada have learned to exploit this fact when hunting marmots, seeking out orange splashes of lichen growing on fouled rock beneath marmot holes. On the coast *Xanthoria* is prolific among sea bird nesting colonies where it enjoys the plentiful supply of bird guano. For this same reason it is found growing on the tops of gravestones far from the sea, enriched by the droppings of birds as they stop to perch.

Above the reach of waves is the pale grey-green band formed of various species including the shrubby, tufted sea ivory *Ramalina siliquosa* and crusts of black shield lichen *Lecanora atra* and parelle *Ochrolechia parella,* a pale grey crust with a distinctive warty appearance.

Solar powered fungi

By now you may be wondering what exactly are lichens and what brings them to the coastal fringe? Although some look rather plant-like in appearance, lichens are actually a partnership of fungi and algae living symbiotically for mutual benefit. Fungi are incapable of making their own food and usually provide for themselves as parasites or decomposers. In the lichen partnership, the fungus is the dominant partner, cultivating its algal companions to manufacture food by photosynthesis. In this process, algae convert water and carbon dioxide into fuel for the fungus and in return, the fungus acts as a protective covering for the algae. Together they can exploit habitats that they would not survive alone. One lichenologist has described lichens as fungi that have discovered agriculture. I like to think of them as fungi with solar panels installed for energy production. Whichever way you visualise it, the partnership is a remarkable one, that has allowed lichens to grow in places too harsh or limited for most other organisms. They are pioneers on bare rock, desert sand, cleared soil, dead wood, animal bones, rusty metal, living bark and are doing rather well on the rubber seal around one of the windows on my camper van.

'Lichens in spaaaaace ...'

The basic physiology of lichens allows them to thrive in extreme environments like the rocky coastal fringe, where for other plants conditions are simply too inhospitable. Because lichens lack roots, they are able to grow on other objects, relying on absorption of water and nutrients throughout their upper surface.

Combined with their ability to shut down metabolically during periods of unfavourable conditions, they have proved to be extremely hardy in the harshest environments on earth. With this knowledge scientists decided to up the stakes and test lichen limits beyond the confines of our planet. In 2005 the European Space Agency exposed specimens of two lichen species to open space for fourteen days before returning them to earth (the lichens were shielded during re-entry to our atmosphere). Despite their exposure to the vacuum of space, cosmic radiation, full-spectrum UV light and intense temperatures the lichens survived and regained normal function soon after their return.

Small Pharma

Collectively lichens are able to produce an arsenal of more than five hundred unique biochemical compounds that enhance their survival in marginal habitats; these serve to control light exposure, repel herbivores, kill attacking microbes and discourage competition from plants. Among them are many pigments and antibiotics that have made lichens useful to people in traditional societies. In Scotland the maritime lichen parelle was used to produce a dye for tweed from its reaction with ammonia. Back-in-the-day, the cheapest source of ammonia was stale urine, resulting in the distinctive smell of old lichen-dyed tweed. More

Parelle forms distinctive grey warty crusts on the rock and in the past were collected for use as a dye.

fascinating was the use of shrubby lichens by the Ancient Egyptians to stuff the body cavities of mummies during preservation.

These days lichen compounds are used in deodorants, herbal tinctures and perfumes, although large-scale harvesting has never taken off due to their very slow growth rate. Many grow less than a millimetre per year and are extremely long-lived; some lichens are thought to be among the oldest living things on earth (around 9,000 years old). This longevity and the fact that they readily absorb atmospheric pollutants mean they are also extremely useful as long-term bio monitors. Studies have shown that the more lichens present in an area the better the air quality, thereby providing a natural indicator of how man-made substances are affecting the environment. I have often kept my magnetism for lichens to myself, unable to explain my fascination with the crusts that cover high-tide rock or hang from tree bark. Lichens are surely one of the most under-rated wonders of the natural world.

Zones between the tides

Below the bands of lichen and only visible at low tide, sedentary marine animals and seaweeds also inhabit the rock in well-defined vertical zones. This area is covered and uncovered by the tide and is called the intertidal because it is between (inter) the tides.

The composition of the different bands here is dictated by the amount of wave action experienced by a particular shore. Along open coasts with plenty of waves, millions of barnacles form a greyish buff swathe just below the black tar lichen. Of the animals fixed to the rock, they live the furthest up the shore meaning they spend several hours of each day exposed to the air. As with many inhabitants living between the tides they have been honed by millions of years of evolution to thrive here in one of the most extreme environments on the planet. In a later chapter we will take a close look at the fascinating life of barnacles. Dotted among the barnacles may be various grazing sea snails including limpets and periwinkles, whose lives we will dip into in the *Sea Snails* chapter.

Beneath the band of barnacles is a dark brown band made up of various species of

The intertidal zone is the area covered and uncovered by the tide (top).

The band of barnacles extending around the coast; dotted among them are limpets and periwinkles (bottom).

brown seaweeds; the wracks. Here we find channel wrack, spiral wrack, bladder wrack and serrated wrack. On sheltered coasts, such as in harbours and sea lochs, barnacles are overgrown and displaced by the seaweeds that grow thick and luxuriant; here egg wrack and

Various species of seaweeds thrive intertidally, especially the brown wracks.

Skomer Head is number 1 on the Ballantine Scale, a bench mark for the most exposed, swell-beaten rocky shores.

horn wrack may be added to the list as they prefer calmer conditions. On both types of shore at the low-water mark, large brown seaweeds called kelp are found with heads bowed awaiting the return of the tide (the next chapter explores the wonderful world of seaweeds). These mark the edge of the truly submerged world that must be visited by swimming.

The Ballantine Scale of exposure

These living vertical bands, though often clearly defined to the eye, represent a complex interaction of factors that include competition for space and food, tolerance to wave action and the drying conditions of being exposed to air, as well as predation and grazing pressure. When analysed it's far from simple, yet the consistent

outcome means we are able to compare shores with similar collections of marine life and deduce how much wave action they experience. This is thanks to the Ballantine Scale. Created by marine biologist Bill Ballantine in 1961, the Ballantine Scale is a "biologically-defined exposure scale for the comparative study of rocky shores" and assigns a particular shore a number from one to eight according to the marine communities living there. By comparing the species living on shores exposed to heavy wave action and those in very sheltered harbour-type habitats, as well as everything in between, he devised the scale to reflect this. To illustrate, a shore classified as one on the Ballantine Scale would experience heavy surf almost continuously and show a dominance of species that are low profile and can hang on, such as barnacles; a shore at eight on the scale is extremely calm and sheltered and shows total seaweed cover and minimal or no barnacle cover.

The benchmark for the Ballantine Scale was Skomer Head, an imposing cliff swathed in black and orange lichens on the west coast of Skomer Island in Pembrokeshire. This was Bill's number one, the most extreme of rocky shores that experiences regular, heavy ocean conditions and is inhabited by a sparse and hardy collection of intertidal animals and seaweeds. I've gazed in awe at its lofty bands of lichen from my sea kayak and various boats over the years. Even on the calmest of summer days it experiences the surge of long-range ocean swells; it's a wild place for sure and bears the broadest stripes with the most tenacious suite of marine life to prove it.

Dr Lou's low-down ... The Ballantine legacy

Following his work on limpets on Pembrokeshire shores and establishing the Ballantine Scale, Bill Ballantine emigrated to New Zealand in 1964, where he was appointed the first director of the University of Auckland's Leigh Marine Laboratory. His subsequent work pioneered establishment of the Marine Reserves Act 1971 and the creation of New Zealand's first marine reserve at Leigh in 1975. Not long after, a 'no take' marine reserve was established at Leigh; both of these initiatives were among the first of their kind world-wide. These efforts ultimately led to the creation of more marine reserves throughout New Zealand and spawned a huge body of scientific literature based on marine reserve research worldwide. Bill's own research focused on the rocky intertidal where he collected one of the longest existing time-series on intertidal reef communities. He also had the foresight to establish daily monitoring of sea surface temperature at Leigh, which continues nearly 50 years later and is providing important insights into climate change in our coastal oceans.

Widely recognised as the father of marine conservation in New Zealand, Bill received a vast range of honours and awards over the years for his work on marine conservation issues. His 1991 book *Marine reserves for New Zealand* grabbed the attention of policy makers and local communities alike, both in New Zealand and overseas. In 1996 he was awarded the Goldman Environmental Prize for work on marine conservation, and in 2002, Bill was awarded the New Zealand Marine Sciences Society Award for his continued outstanding contribution to marine science in New Zealand. Bill travelled to many countries, giving public lectures and running workshops, all focused on the key message that no-take marine reserves are a crucial tool for protecting marine biodiversity. Within New Zealand, he inspired NGOs, local communities and schools to put forward proposals for marine reserves. He continued to champion marine reserves well into his retirement until his passing in 2015. The Ballantine legacy will continue for generations to come, growing stronger with every patch of ocean granted protection.

There are more than 700 species of seaweed species in the UK, some of which create important and beautiful habitats underwater.

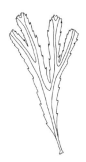

Seaweeds

Seaweeds are plant-like organisms that generally live attached to rock or other firm substrates in coastal areas. Often referred to as marine macroalgae – they can be described as just that – large algae living in the sea. They vary in size from the fifty-metre-long giant kelps of California to others growing as crusts on the rock just a few millimetres thick. There are more than 700 species in UK waters that are classified into three groups according to their colour; green, red or brown. These colours are produced by the pigment that is most dominant in their tissues and are used to capture light energy from the sun to make food during photosynthesis. In this way they are similar to land plants but that is where it ends; they lack the complex vascular and root system of land plants and do not produce flowers or seeds for reproduction. Instead they simply absorb the nutrients they need through their surface tissues and reproduce by forming spores, as well as regeneration from fragments of the parent plant.

1 The fluid form of seaweeds yields to the movement of water.

2 Gas-filled bladders provide buoyancy that lifts the frond up into the water column towards the light.

3 With no water to hold them aloft, intertidal seaweeds flop on to the shore at low tide in slippery heaps.

4 Sea lettuce grows leafy like a bright green lettuce and is in fact good to eat.

5 Gutweed forms strings of inflated tubes and is often found in rockpools high up the shore.

6 Pink paint weed forms crusts on the rock much like a lichen, that merge together to form a chalky veneer.

7 The stiff, chalky fronds of coral weed are suitably unpalatable to grazers seen here in a rockpool among pink paint weed.

Fluid strength

The structural strength of seaweeds relies on them being fluid and flexible in a dynamic environment. With water being denser than air they get the support they need from the water itself as well as gas-filled bladders and tissues that hold them vertically in the water column. At low tide they flop on the shore in great piles that help to conserve moisture, yet when the tide returns, they are lifted into vertical gardens. Studies have recorded water movements in seaweed beds equivalent to 900 mile per hour winds on the land. Large, rigid supportive structures would not survive this sort of treatment for long. Instead seaweeds are floppy and yielding and have developed extreme torsional strength, meaning they are able to endure heavy twisting forces that result from surging water and breaking waves. Seaweeds also form an important habitat providing food and shelter for many marine animals. They are also used by humans in all sorts of food products and cosmetics, including toothpaste and shampoo, as well as for fertilisers.

Green seaweeds

The most common representative of green seaweeds is sea lettuce *Ulva lactuca* often seen in rock pools growing on the rock or the backs of limpets. As the name suggests it is a bright green, leafy seaweed that is good to eat. Another common and closely related seaweed is gutweed *Ulva intestinalis*. This one is elongated and irregularly tubular in structure much like a bright green inflated intestine, hence the Latin name. Both thrive where limpets and grazing snails have been denied access, for example pools very high up the shore or where a fresh water stream runs down the beach.

Limpet fodder

Whenever I arrive at a shore to be presented with a green swathe of these seaweeds I like to hypothesise why. When the *Sea Empress* oil tanker spilled 72,000 tonnes of crude oil and 370 tonnes of heavy fuel oil into the sea around Pembrokeshire in 1994 many limpets on the shores were killed. What followed was a greening of the shores as the sporelings of green seaweeds that would normally be eaten were able to flourish into full grown plants. The whole appearance and ecology of the shore changed until the limpet population recovered. Both gutweed and sea lettuce are summer annuals meaning that they both die off at the end of the summer. Once the limpet population recovered, the ecology of the shore returned to how it was before the spill, demonstrating the key role of limpets in shore ecology.

Red seaweeds

Painting the insides of rockpools and any wet channels and crevices pink are a collection of red seaweeds. Instead of growing leafy like many other seaweeds they form crusts on the rock that join up to form a paint-like veneer. They belong to a sub-group of red seaweeds called *Corallinaceae* that are characterised by cell walls hardened by calcium deposits. This makes them rather coral-like, hence *Corallinaceae*, and resistant to the grazing snails that are put off by the chalky texture. They are confined to wet or damp areas as they must remain moist; if they dry out they bleach bright white. Another member of this group you are likely to see in rockpools is coral weed *Corallina officinalis* – a tufted pink and white seaweed.

With its strong, garlicky flavour pepper dulse is one of my favourite culinary seaweeds.

Many red seaweeds tend to be small and require the use of a hand lens to observe their finer features; it is certainly worth the effort as many are beautiful in their intricate detail. One of my favourite red seaweeds is pepper dulse *Osmundea pinnatifida,* mostly because of its strong fiery flavour. It is small with flattened branches that are rather rubbery in texture. The colour varies widely from golden yellow through deep red to brown so dark it appears black. It is found in the middle to low shore and prefers water conditions that are neither too tame nor too lively. I have enjoyed many afternoons out on the water or wandering along the shore with the flavour repeating on me for hours to come.

Brown seaweeds

Belonging to the brown seaweeds are the large wracks and kelps. These are common and easily identifiable species that are worth getting to know and will launch you confidently on your seaweed identification journey.

Wracks

The wracks are a collection of six familiar seaweeds found on intertidal rocks and cliffs. They are common and accessible on an average low tide and have simple and distinctive features that enable easy identification. The term wrack derives from Old English meaning wreck or ruin, as they look wrecked upon the shore at low water. Though classified together as brown seaweeds they often appear almost black or glow a rich golden-yellow. Observed with a discerning eye, these dark, slippery hanks materialise as different species separated into bands of varying heights above the water line. Much like the coastal lichens (page 19) they show a distinct vertical zonation determined by a host of factors that includes tolerance to drying in the air.

In addition to vertical differences their distribution is also affected by how exposed

a particular shore is to wave action. Certain species are excluded from shores pounded by waves due to their fragile growth form and are only seen at locations where calmness prevails. Knowing that horned wrack, for example, only occurs in sheltered, brackish environments will aid identification.

The following is a guide to the wracks of UK shores and a challenge to go and find them for yourself.

COMMON WRACKS OF UK COASTS:

Channel wrack: *Pelvetia canaliculata*

Found high up the shore towards the high-water mark this is the smallest, hardiest member of the wracks. Hot sun and drying wind may dehydrate this small seaweed to a crisp and snow and ice encrust its fronds, yet each returning tide revitalises it. Common with all marine organisms, time spent in the air is inherently stressful and this particular seaweed shows some impressive adaptations to deal with such lengthy exposure. Living at the high-water mark like this may mean waiting 12 hours before the tide returns, while seaweed anchored in the middle of the shore would be re-submerged in half the time.

Of all the seaweeds channel wrack grows the highest above the waterline and may dry to a crisp before the tide returns (below).

Channel wrack is beautifully crafted into gutter-shaped fronds that hold moisture (right) ...

... which may freeze solid in winter (left).

You may ask why not choose the easy life and grow where conditions are kinder? In an environment where you need to be well anchored to survive, space is at a premium and competition is fierce; the ability to survive in more testing conditions opens the door to some exclusive real estate. The response is a remarkable ability to tolerate dehydration; studies have shown that it is able to lose more than ninety percent of its water content and quickly return to normal function on re-immersion. Recent discoveries have shown that channel wrack hosts a fungus within its tissues that may be responsible for its extreme resilience to drying. Of less relevance but certainly noteworthy and memorable is the Latin name *Pelvetia canaliculata*, that although referring to the frond channels, suggests something entirely different when mispronounced, "can-I-lick-u-later".

ID TOP TIPS:
- Found high up the shore among tar lichen
- Gutter-like channels in frond

Once the tide returns channel wrack rehydrates to its former golden glory.

Surface living

Plants that grow on the surface of other plants merely for support, while gaining nutrients and food from their surroundings, are called epiphytes. Similarly, animals growing attached to any surface including plants are called epifauna. Some of the larger brown seaweeds support a rich community of both seaweeds and animals living as epiphytes and epifauna on their surfaces.

Spiralled wrack: *Fucus spiralis*

Growing just below channel wrack on the shore spiralled wrack is characterised by the way its frond forms a loose spiral. This is most obvious when the frond is held between the thumb and forefingers and allowed to hang in the air. Some fronds have bulbous ends that resemble gas bladders. These are in fact the reproductive bodies called receptacles. Observed closely these structures are dotted all over but have a distinct, smooth rim that is characteristic of this species.

ID TOP TIPS:

- Frond forms a loose spiral
- Grows just below channel wrack
- Rounded receptacles have a distinct rim

Egg or knotted wrack: *Ascophyllum nodosum*

The thin, strappy fronds appear knotted with large oval gas bladders (hence egg or knotted wrack), and are unable to withstand the rigours of wave-exposed coasts. The long, luxuriant growths are suited to more sheltered shores and grow abundantly along estuaries. They may also be found growing in sheltered corners of semi-exposed shores. Small dark tufts of red seaweed are often found growing epiphytically on this seaweed using it as a platform to gain elevation towards the light. You can have fun ageing these seaweeds by counting the number of bladders that run sequentially along the length of the main frond starting at the holdfast. Each bladder represents one year of growth and may reach fifteen in sheltered, estuarine habitats.

ID TOP TIPS:

- Oval bladders
- Long, thin strap-like fronds

Spiralled wrack grows high up the shore and has a loosely twisted frond (left).

Thin strappy fronds and egg-shaped gas bladders are signs you have found egg wrack.

Bladder wrack: *Fucus vesiculosus*

An iconic seaweed of the seashore, bladder wrack grows just below spiral wrack and a touch below or alongside egg wrack on the vertical zonation scale. It has a flattened frond with a thick rib running along its length. At intervals and laying either side of this midrib lie pairs of small, rounded gas bladders. The buoyancy of the bladders in water floats the frond up towards the sunlight on which it depends as energy source.

On shores where wave action is heavy but moderate enough to still allow its survival,

bladder wrack modifies its growth form. In such places the gas bladders are absent, and the frond takes on a spindly, gaunt appearance that is quite different to the lush fronds seen on other shores.

By reducing its surface area and buoyancy bladder wrack provides less resistance to heavier water movement, enabling it to survive in a more extreme habitat. Identification of these modified individuals becomes a process of elimination of the other wracks according to their defining features. Some individuals may have reproductive swellings at the ends of the fronds similar to spiral wrack. However, when observed closely they lack the distinct smooth rim of spiral wrack.

ID TOP TIPS:
- Paired, round gas bladders
- Thickened 'midrib'

The pert gas bladders of bladder wrack (top).

The exposed form of bladder wrack lacks gas bladders and takes on a tough, lean appearance (left).

Underwater the fronds are buoyed up by the gas bladders (below).

Serrated or saw wrack: *Fucus serratus*

This is the easiest wrack to identify due to the deeply serrated edge to the frond and thickened midrib. It grows further still towards the low water mark, often in luxuriant stands that form a thick carpet over rocks at low tide. Though it lacks gas bladders and is extremely floppy, its frond has inherent buoyancy that allows it to float vertically in the water column. Snorkelling among a gently swaying swathe of saw wrack, with shafts of sunlight setting it alight, is one of my favourite mid-summer activities.

ID TOP TIPS:
- Saw-tooth edge to frond
- Obvious 'midrib'

The distinctive saw-tooth edge of serrated wrack makes it instantly recognisable; the tiny white hairs mark the reproductive structures beneath (top).

The inherent buoyancy of serrated wrack's fronds lifts them up from the seabed (middle).

Horned or estuary wrack: *Fucus ceranoides*

This distinctive wrack is confined to the shelter of harbours and estuaries where there is fresh water influence. The branching of the frond forms pairs of horns that together produce a broad fan-shape that is unmistakeable. Though they lack air bladders the edges of the fronds are often inflated along their length to the extent that they stand quite erect at low water.

ID TOP TIPS:
- Characteristic of estuarine habitat where there is freshwater run-off
- Horns in a fan-shape

Horned wrack in Solva harbour (below).

Kelps

Growing furthest down the shore and only un-covered and visible on the lowest spring tides are the kelps. One of my greatest pleasures in life is to glide beneath the sea surface into a forest of kelp glowing in the sunlight. These underwater forests have the same majestic calm as ancient land forests and may extend for thousands of kilometres below the surface. Along Norwegian coasts alone they form a vibrant swathe that covers 5,200 square kilometres of seabed. Found below the lowest tide line on rock, kelps grow large and luxuriant beyond the reach of heavy wave action. Their need for plentiful sunlight, high nutrients and a hard surface on which to grow confine them to shallow, temperate and sub-polar seas worldwide. Here cool, nutrient-rich water is pushed up from the depths producing kelp forests that are one of the most productive and dynamic ecosystems on Earth.

Forests of the sea

Kelps are the largest and most dramatic of all brown seaweeds and there are roughly 100 species worldwide. Those that thrive in UK and European waters tend to form glades or parks, while in other regions of the world, such as north-west America, giant kelps grow into towering underwater forests spanning more than fifty metres in height. These immense seaweeds are the fastest growing organism on earth with a growth rate of sixty centimetres per day. Though they may vary in size all kelp species are based on the same structural plan that comprises four parts. The frond or lamina is the flat leafy area for nutrient uptake and photosynthesis, while the stipe is the stem that provides a lofty, vertical framework for the frond. Some of the giant kelp species also have a pneumatocyst, a gas-filled bladder that forms at the base of the frond such as the bull kelp of British Columbia and Alaska. This kelp is like a moored buoy, the long flexible stipe tethering the crown of fronds to the seabed and the pneumatocyst providing buoyancy to the frond to maximise light capture. Buoyed-up kelps often form dense beds parallel to the shore and are visible at all states of the tide. Finally, the holdfast anchors the kelp to the seabed and though they often look root-like they play no part in nutrient absorption. The structure and extent of the individual parts vary between species and produce some truly beautiful and bizarre forms. The bonus of such distinctive features means that identification often comes with ease.

1 Kelps form complex, highly productive habitats underwater.

2 The flat leafy frond of the kelp absorbs both sunlight and nutrients for photosynthesis.

3 The stipe and holdfast provide structure and anchorage to the seabed.

4 Bull kelp of the northwest Pacific coasts have gas bladders at the base of the frond and create huge floating rafts at the surface.

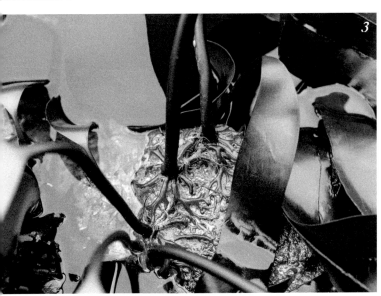

KELPS OF UK COASTS:

Furbelows: *Saccorhiza polyschides*

Annual seaweed which grows rapidly up to 2.5m in length and can grow up to 2m in a month. It has a bulky, bulbous holdfast that is hollow and warty and clings to the rock by claw-like extensions. The stipe is flat with a deeply pleated edge at its base, hence furbelows, which is a pleated border of a skirt. The frond is also divided into strap-like fingers. Being short-lived it is often found washed up on beaches in huge piles providing interesting beach combing during winter and a whole other habitat for strandline communities. As it rots down, the nutrients locked up in its tissues are released back to the ocean for the next generation of seaweeds to thrive on. Intertidal.

Sugar kelp or sea belt: *Saccharina latissima*

Annual seaweed growing up to 1.5m in length with a claw-like holdfast, short flexible stipe and undivided, broad frond with ruffled edges and characteristic dimples. This is a glorious seaweed to behold and tastes delicious too. Intertidal.

Furbelows have a flat stipe and warty holdfast that clings to the rock (top left).

The frills of sugar kelp (above).

Dabberlocks: *Alaria esculenta*

Perennial that can live up to 7 years and grows up to 1.5m in length. Spear-shaped membranous frond with a distinct midrib that grows from a flexible stipe and attached via a claw-like holdfast. The elongated leafy outgrowths at the base of the frond are reproductive structures and are delicious to eat. Dabberlocks are subtidal (live below the average low tide mark) and only seen on extremely low spring tides.

Oarweed or tangle: *Laminaria digitata*

A perennial that lives 6–10 years and grows up to 1.5m long with a leathery sheet-like frond that splits into broad straps; the stipe is smooth, slightly oval in cross-section and floppy when out of water at low tide. Intertidal.

Oarweed has a leathery frond that splits into straps and has a smooth stipe (top right).

The spear-shaped Dabberlocks (right).

Forest kelp or northern kelp:
Laminaria hyperborea

A perennial that lives more than 10 years and grows from 0.5–3m high with a leathery sheet-like frond that splits into broad straps; the stipe is rough, round in cross-section and stiff so that it stands erect at extreme low tide. The stipe also often has a thick covering of seaweeds and other life growing on it. Subtidal and only seen on extremely low spring tides.

Forest kelp underwater (top) ... and exposed on a huge equinoctial spring low tide (bottom).

Forest riches

I clambered down the rocks to the water's edge and pulled on fins, snorkel and mask to complete my snorkeling attire, then eased myself into the water. Finning out for deeper water I hung over a dense stand of kelp, its fronds forming a tangled rug of bronzed ribbons, luminous in the shafting sunlight. The urge to dive took me so I drew breath and hinged at the waist allowing my head to lead the plunge, then straightened my legs in a slow spearing to the depths. I pushed down through the loose canopy so that I was in among the stems of the kelp; as thick as broom handles, these spar-like stipes hold the fronds aloft towards the life-giving sunlight pouring down from above. Each was rough and furred with seaweeds, bryozoans and hydroids, a small habitat in itself. I grasped one to anchor myself against the buoyant draw of my wetsuit, testing its grip to the rock.

Ensconced in seaweed I had a fish-eye view of life in a kelp forest, elaborately decorated in autumnal hues and bustling with invertebrate life.

Kelp forests world-wide support an extraordinary amount of life. Their phenomenal capacity for growth (some of the giant kelp species grow up to half a metre per day) combined with their collective architectural complexity allows them to provide a home for a large number of other species. Fish, seals, sea lions, sea otters, crabs, lobsters, sea urchin and many more take shelter and forage for food among them, while hundreds of species of seaweed and invertebrates crowd the surface of each kelp plant. Some graze directly on the kelp like the blue-rayed limpet, *Patella pellucida*, that uses its rough tongue to rasp trails in the frond. Other animals live upon the surface in colonies forming sheets that filter plankton from the water; collectively they are called epifauna and include bryozoans, hydroids and sponges. Seaweeds that grow upon the surface of kelps are epiphytes (see boxed text "Surface living") and form an especially diverse community on the rough stipe of forest kelp.

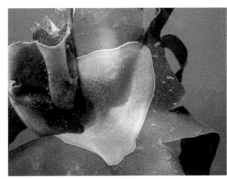

Kelps support all sorts of marine life from tiny blue-rayed limpets (left) ... to spider crabs (below) ... and epifauna like this bryozoan colony (top).

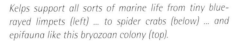

Weedy real estate

Frond, stipe and holdfast each have their own appeal to potential inhabitants. The holdfast, for example, attracts a much more diverse community to its cosy holes and crevices than the two-dimensional flats of the frond. Upwards of 170 species have been recorded living in a single kelp holdfast and a study of oarweed growing along the Norwegian coast found an average of almost 8,000 individual animals per plant. Many of these were mobile, shrimp-like creatures scurrying around in search of tasty morsels or snails grazing on epiphytic seaweeds. The highest densities of these were found on the stipe during summer when epiphytic seaweeds were lush and plentiful and harboured up to 80,000 animals per stipe at their most abundant. Such diversity and plenty rival the most productive ecosystems on the land.

While exploring along the coast, we often see kelps as a tangle of slippery fronds and snaky stipes, marooned and draped on the shore. Viewed underwater they are lifted into glorious stands of golden streamers that sway and dance in the sunlit swell and team with life. In summer I look forward to days when the water is calm and clear enough to swim among them and slip wetsuit-clad beneath the canopy. In the gloom of winter, it is these days of drifting through forests of luminous kelp that fill my waking dreams. The ocean's submerged forests are truly one of the great wonders of the world.

Dr Lou's low-down ... Light in the ocean

Light penetrates through water 2,000 times less than through air, yet both air and water are commonly regarded as transparent and colourless media. The properties of seawater clearly have a drastic effect on the behaviour of light in the sea and by studying this behaviour we can learn much about where marine life flourishes and why.

The dependence of plants on light for photosynthesis means that light will limit plant growth underwater far more than on land. As sunlight shines down onto the ocean's surface some is reflected and does not enter the ocean. That which penetrates the surface is diminished by a process called attenuation through absorption and conversion to other forms of energy, such as heat that warms or evaporates the water, or is used by plants to fuel photosynthesis. Sunlight that is not absorbed can be scattered by molecules and particulates suspended in the water. Scattered light is deflected along new paths and may eventually be either absorbed or directed upward and out of the water towards our eyes. It is this upward-scattered light and the light reflected from particles that determine the colour of the oceans as seen from above.

The growing gloom that accompanies increasing water depth is created by the combined effects of dissolved salts, organic substances, and suspended particles. In the clearest ocean waters only about one percent of the surface light remains at a depth of 150 metres (500 feet) and no sunlight penetrates below a thousand metres. It's this rapid tailing-off of light that limits the distribution of sea-weeds, plants and plant plankton to the upper, light-bathed regions of our oceans. The story does not end there though, as not only do light levels decrease with depth but so do the wave-lengths present in the solar spectrum. We know from our enjoyment of rainbows and school physics lessons that sunlight or solar radiation is made up of a delightful spectrum of coloured light. These colours reduce in density at different rates. Both short wavelengths (ultraviolet) and long wavelengths (infrared) are absorbed rapidly and are not available for scattering. Only blue-green wavelengths penetrate to any depth, and because the blue-green light is most available for scattering, the oceans appear blue to the human eye. However, not all sea water appears blue. Coastal waters of UK coasts are often emerald green or brown after stormy weather. The explanation lies in the size and type of particles suspended in the water, as well as the concentration of organic substances dissolved in it. Coastal waters tend to have many more micro-organisms, detritus and run-off from the land, all of which tend to absorb blue light more strongly and give the water a more organic hue.

To a seaweed or plant underwater the light available for photosynthesis may be highly variable in both intensity and colour spectrum. As a result, the pigments used by seaweeds to capture light for photosynthesis show a diversity not seen in land plants; their sumptuous diversity of colours reflect this. Though all seaweeds possess the green pigment chloro-phyll, their dominant pigments provide the colour we see. Phycoerythrin is the dominant pigment in many red seaweeds and reflects red wavelengths of light and absorbs blue, while in brown seaweeds the superior pigment fucox-anthin masks the other pigments present and reflects yellow light. If you've ever been lucky enough to swim in a kelp forest lit up by the sun you will attest to the golden yellow hues of its fucoxanthin. Formerly it was thought that seaweed species had adapted to their habitat by having pigments that were sensitive to the different wavelengths of the light spectrum. In this way they could take advantage of precisely that part of the spectrum reaching the depths at which they lived. For example, the blue and violet wavelengths penetrate to greater depths. The red seaweed that live in these waters do indeed contain pigments that absorb blue and violet light and, as a consequence, appear to have the complementary colour red. Alas, experiments have since shown that this otherwise elegant relationship does not always hold true; nature is consistent only in its thrilling complexity.

Barnacles thrive on the wave swept rocky shores of our coasts.

Barnacles

It's safe to say that barnacles have mastered the wave-swept, intertidal margins of the world's rocky coasts. Here they thrive in their millions in one of the most hostile environments on the planet. Though true inhabitants of the ocean, on the shore the water visits intermittently with the ebb and flow of the tide, exposing them to the full rigours of life in air. Fixed to the rock they endure the heaviest anti-cyclonic storms, swelter under the summer sun, get dowsed in rainwater and at times may become smothered by a freezing veneer of snow and ice. All this on a regular daily, lunar and seasonal cycle. Their merit was recognised by Charles Darwin who spent eight years carrying out a detailed study of barnacles or Cirripedia, the 'curly-footed' crustaceans that glue themselves to surfaces for a living. As we will learn these hardy, ubiquitous relatives of crabs and lobsters were certainly worthy of history's most famous biologist's attention.

Cosmopolitan curly-foots

There are over a thousand species of barnacles worldwide, distributed from the poles to the tropics. Their habits are as diverse as their varied forms. There are those that live attached solely to humpback whales and turtles and have a shell of hard, chalky plates covering their soft

Acorn barnacles (top).

Volcano barnacles grow on rock (bottom).

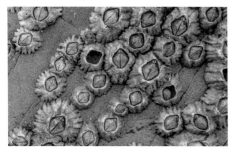

bodies, while others burrow into shells of molluscs or coral, or are parasitic in crabs, and lack the hard carapace of other barnacles. Instead their peculiar soft, sac-like or root-like body (in the case of the parasitic barnacles) is protected by the hard surface into which they have burrowed or the body of their crab host. More familiar are those that live attached to intertidal rock in great swathes, the acorn and volcano barnacles or, as with the common goose barnacle, *Lepas anatifera*, settles on objects floating in open ocean currents. Size-wise they vary from the tiny burrowing barnacle which grows just a few millimetres across to the giant acorn barnacle *Balanus nubilus* of north-west Pacific coasts which spans a whopping fifteen centimetres in diameter.

Pollicipes pollicipes is a chunky goose barnacle with a thick stalk found growing along the Atlantic coast of west Europe. It is prized for its superior flavour and on Spanish restaurant menus goes by the name of 'percebes'. Its habit of growing on rock at the extreme reaches of low tide in some of the most surf-rich areas of Europe means collecting them is the vocation of the brave. In Galicia, north-west Spain, the *percebeiros* harvest them by hand under

Common goose barnacles attach to floating objects that often get beached (top).

Percebes, or goose barnacles, growing on rock in Galicia, Spain (bottom).

strict control by the authorities, ensuring the sustainable nature of the fishery. The frequency of large waves that wash their preferred habitat also affords them some protection from over-collection and brings a regular supply of plankton for them to feed on.

Upside-down crustaceans in a box

All barnacles begin life as larvae swimming among the ocean plankton. They then settle onto a suitable hard surface such as rock, the tail fluke of a humpback whale or for some, the shell of a particular species of crab. At this point they glue their heads to the preferred surface using an adhesive superior to any man-made preparation, and then undergo complete metamorphosis into the adult form. From this moment on they spend the rest of their lives anchored to the same spot. In the case of the more familiar acorn barnacles and goose barnacles, they then begin to form a hard shell around their soft bodies.

The shell they form around themselves is made up of different plates, some of which remain articulated and form a small door to the outside world. This allows the doors to open and the feathery cirri or 'curly feet' to be extended into the water to sieve plankton for sustenance. When the tide is out, or a predator threatens, the doors are sealed tightly shut against the outside world, retaining enough moisture for survival and protecting their soft bodies from predation.

When covered by the tide barnacles open up their trap doors and extend the feathery legs to feed (above).

Recently settled juvenile barnacles nestled into space among adult barnacles (right).

Disposable super-penis

In the case of the intertidal acorn barnacle, their most impressive attribute exists in the reproductive arena, as they are extremely well endowed. These tiny crustaceans boast the super-penis of the natural world; by proportion they have the largest penis in the animal kingdom. At roughly eight times the length of their own bodies, you may question the merits of such excessive proportions until you remember that these sedentary cirripeds cannot roam in search of a mate. Instead they use their extremely long and mobile penis to blindly reach into their neighbour's shell to deposit sperm. This short extract from Charles Darwin's epic, two-volume tome *A monograph of the subclass Cirripedia* celebrates his fascination with barnacles and their awesome penises:

"The males are attached at a considerable distance from the orifice of the sack of the female, into which the spermatozoa have to be conveyed; and to effect this, the prosci-formed penis is wonderfully developed, so that in Cryptophialus, when fully extended, it must equal between eight and nine times the entire length of the animal!"

Adding a further dimension to the wonder, a fascinating study by two Canadian biologists showed that penis dimensions vary according to how much wave action a particular habitat is exposed. Barnacles living in wave swept environments had relatively shorter, stouter penises compared to those living in sheltered areas where calm conditions were conducive to a bit of extra length. Other studies have shown that once it has served its purpose the redundant appendage is discarded and regrown the next season; with something so oversized and with limited space inside their tiny shells this makes perfect sense.

Strategy: small and hard or big and floppy?

Barnacles living in the intertidal are constrained by their rigidity; there is a limit to the size of something that confronts the waves. Their strategy for survival is to grow small with a hard shell in the form of a cone so as to present minimal resistance to moving water. The opposite is true of seaweeds that flourish in their flexibility, yielding to water movement with their flowing forms. Their strategy enables them to grow much larger than their intertidal animal counterparts; two captivating, divergent solutions to the same problem. With a fossil record stretching back 500 million years barnacle design has clearly been honed to perfection, having allowed them to survive the last four mass extinction events. In these changing times, it's reassuring to know that they were here long before any of us first glimpsed the ocean and will likely be around long after we are laid to rest.

Back in my university days I was observing some barnacles feeding under a low power microscope, enjoying the close-up view of the shells parting and the legs unfurling to strain plankton. Suddenly a long white thread popped out from between the legs and reached towards a neighbouring barnacle. It was surprisingly quick and mobile, rapidly coiling in and out of the shell. I quickly realised this lithe appendage was the much-revered barnacle penis and I was over-joyed at seeing one in action for the first time. Since then I have enlightened many people to the ways and proportions of the barnacle penis, yet this remains the only time I have seen one for myself.

The barnacle penis is extremely long and mobile in order to reach and fertilise female barnacles.

Dr Lou's low-down ...

The parasitic barnacle *Sacculina carcini* differs greatly from other barnacles. While the swimming larval form is typical of other barnacles, the adult form is reduced to a collection of tissues that resembles a microscopic slug. Their most common hosts are young shore crabs *Carcinus maenus,* and it is only female swimming larvae that infect the crabs. When a larva finds a suitable host, it penetrates the shell of the crab via one of the antennae and grows tendrils throughout the host's body that allow it to obtain nutrients from the crab's tissues. As it develops, it produces a mass of reproductive tissue, visible as a sac-like lump on the crab's abdomen. The male barnacle on the other hand is microscopic, and lives permanently attached to a female barnacle in order to fertilise her eggs. Apart from the nutritional benefits gained, the parasite barnacle also modifies the host's behaviour in a couple of unsettling ways. Firstly, if the parasitised crab is male it becomes feminised, whereby its gonads and fighting claws shrink and it grows a larger abdomen. Infected crabs then all act as females, incubating and caring for the parasites eggs as if they were its own, much like a songbird nurturing the egg and young of an invasive cuckoo. The eggs are incubated in the abdomen of the crab host until they hatch into larvae. The parasitised crabs then climb to high places with fast currents and disperse larval parasites like they would their own eggs, thus continuing the cycle of infection. The parasite also prevents the crab from moulting its carapace thereby hindering growth.

This top shell enjoys a herbivorous diet of algae and tiny seaweeds.

Sea Snails

Sea snails make up just a small part of the impressive mollusc phylum, one of the most diverse groups of animals on the planet. With more than 85,000 species, Mollusca include creatures as wildly different as sea slugs, octopi and mussels. They come in a bewildering range of sizes, from microscopic to more than twenty metres long in the case of the giant squid *Architeuthis*. Their common thread is a soft body after which they are named; *molluscus* means soft in Latin. Most molluscs also have a shell, which affords protection to their soft bodies, though some have lost it over the course of evolution. All have a mantle – a fold in the body wall that secretes the calcium carbonate of which the shell is made. Their varied forms are as diverse as the habitats they choose and the ways in which they nourish themselves. There are those that sit and lick rock or seaweed, rasping a thin layer of greens for sustenance. Others with more carnivorous tastes bore through the shells of other animals to get at the flesh, or actively hunt mobile prey with prehensile arms that feed their catch into beak-like jaws.

This chapter focuses on the shelled sea snails most commonly seen along UK shores. Snails are some of the most familiar molluscs and are especially widespread in the marine environment. Many are herbivorous, enjoying a plant-based diet that is scraped and rasped off using the rough tongue called a radula. Limpets, top shells and periwinkles fall into this category and spend countless hours grazing over rock and seaweed. Others, like the whelks, are flesh eaters and employ a different approach to secure a meal.

The octopus (left), mussel (top) and sea slug (middle) all belong to the soft-bodied Mollusca along with sea snails.

Herbivores

The rock lickers

Limpets belong to the most primitive group of living snails and the oldest fossils date back to the Middle Ordovician period (471–462 million years ago). These marine snails lead fascinating lives under the protection of a robust, exceptionally streamlined, conical shell. Though often seen stationary as though fixed permanently to the spot, they actually move freely on their muscular foot much like a garden snail. As they glide along, they lick the rock with their radula, audible to those with a keen ear as a rhythmic rasping. This action removes a fine layer of algae and seaweed sporelings from the rock and plays a critical role in maintaining the structure and balance of all other species in the shore community. Their key role was grimly illustrated by the Sea Empress oil spill in February 1996, which covered the shores of Pembrokeshire in oil, killing many limpets. The change that followed was remarkable – the intertidal area

bloomed bright green as the lack of limpets allowed sporelings of seaweed that would otherwise have been grazed to reach full growth. Amazingly within a few years the limpets had returned, and restored balance to the shore.

Interestingly limpets do not graze over the top of each other's shells and cannot reach over the top of their own shells with the radula; as a consequence they are often seen wearing a luxuriant growth of seaweeds like a living head-dress. In calm conditions the seaweed can reach quite a length, causing extra drag for the limpet in moving water and demonstrating what the rest of the shore might look like if the limpets were removed.

Roaming and homing

Following a feeding jaunt, each limpet will return to a home position on the rock, using invisible trails to navigate. This ability to find their way back 'home' continues to puzzle limpet biologists despite decades of study. Experiments have been carried out to try and discern how the homing instinct functions. Researchers have set up physical barriers and chemical cordons on rocks to prevent limpets returning to their home positions by the same route as they left.

Limpets use their rough tongue called a radula to rasp algae from the rock (top).

Seaweeds grow rather well on the shells of limpets, beyond the reach of their rasping radulas (bottom).

Yet the limpets slowly by-pass any hindrance, proving that not only can they navigate back home, but that they can do so without retracing their original track. The rigours of autumn on the rocky shore provide limpets with some of their greatest life challenges as relentless waves pound and tug at their shells. Various tactics are employed to prevent dislodgement. For example, studies have shown that while foraging at higher states of the tide they use suction; this provides strong attachment and good resistance to the hydrodynamic lift of moving water, while still allowing the limpet to glide across the seabed. At low tide, there is no need for suction as the limpets are in air; instead they use the glue-like adhesion of the sticky foot-mucous to bond to the rock.

Life at the home scar

Their most ingenious tactic, though, is the method used to achieve the supremely tight seal between the rim of their shell and the rock at their home base. This is achieved in one of two ways. The limpet either grinds its shell to the shape of the rock (in the case of very hard rock such as granite), or the rock conforms to the shape of the shell rim on slate or shale rock types. The outcome is a uniquely perfect seal which traps life-giving moisture inside the shell when the tide is out, preventing them from drying out, and providing a real challenge to predators to separate shell from rock. Vacant home scars are often visible on soft rocks or

areas where there has been a dense covering of encrusting life-forms on surrounding rock. Residents are either out getting their fill of algae or have been unlucky victims of predation by birds such as oystercatchers. These striking birds march around limpet covered rocks at low tide methodically tapping at shells testing for a suitable gap between rock and shell rim. On finding a cocked rim the oystercatcher gets to work chiselling and prizing until the limpet is able to be flipped and the juicy flesh beneath revealed.

A limpet sits tight in its precisely carved home scar (top).

Empty home scars carved into soft shale (bottom).

Jewels among the kelp fronds

Autumn is an important time for the blue-rayed limpet *Patella pellucida*. These small, vibrantly coloured creatures are cousins of shore limpets. They graze on brown seaweeds and are often found bejewelling the fronds of kelp with their blue-striped, shiny opal shells.

Like leaf-fall from deciduous trees on the land, kelps shed their flailing fronds in autumn to reduce drag during stormy seas and to rid themselves of accumulating epifauna and flora (other seaweeds and animals growing on their surface – see boxed text 'Surface living' on page 30). Falling temperatures thus signal the limpet to migrate from the fronds, down the kelp stipe to the refuge of the bulbous holdfast clamped to the seabed. Here they spend the winter awaiting new growth and spring's cue to begin their return journey to the upper reaches of the kelp.

A plethora of periwinkles

Other vegetarian snails commonly found on UK shores include the periwinkles and top shells. Nestled in the crevices of rock painted black by tar lichen can be found scores of tiny sea snails, the smallest of which is the small or grape-pip periwinkle *Melarhaphe neritoides*. Literally the size of a grape pip or smaller you would be forgiven for never having noticed them; a little lower down the shore they are often found tucked into empty barnacle shells. They feed on black lichen and organic matter, which is licked from the rock with their rough tongue-like radula. Between autumn and spring during high tides and storms the females release floating fertilised egg capsules. After a few weeks drifting in open water, swimming larvae hatch from the eggs to feed on the plankton. After a further few weeks they settle into

Blue-rayed limpets grazing on kelp fronds.

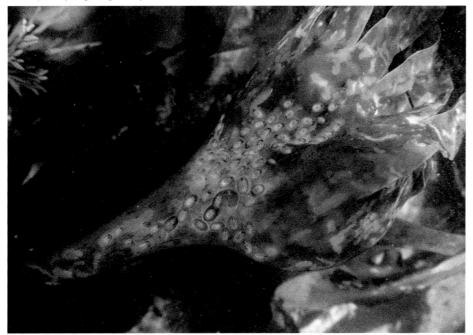

crevices high up the shore and undergo metamorphosis into miniature versions of the adult. The requirement for sea splash to disperse their eggs means black periwinkles are only found on exposed, wave-washed stretches of coast; harbour life is too tame for this snail.

Alongside and travelling further down the shore than the small periwinkles are rough periwinkles *Littorina saxatilis*; these grow larger in size and have distinct ridges on the shell. They also lick rock for sustenance but have a different strategy when it comes to reproduction. Instead of releasing the eggs to an ocean of hungry mouths, the female retains

the eggs inside her shell; they then hatch out as fully-formed minute winkles. This is parental care periwinkle style. Both species of periwinkle are accustomed to spending many hours out of the water; their gills are reduced and a cavity within their body is modified to function as a lung. In very dry conditions they will glue themselves to the rock and withdraw into their shell sealing it shut. They will then go into a

state of torpor until conditions become more favourable. Living in among the wracks is the flat periwinkle *Littorina obtusata* that relies on superior camouflage for a quiet life of grazing. The rounded shape of the shell and its olive green to yellow or brown colouration mimic the gas bladders of bladder wrack superbly. They lay their eggs on seaweed – these hatch into miniature crawling versions of the adults.

Small periwinkles are tiny sea snails that live high up the shore among the black tar lichen (below).

Often found nestled among barnacles, rough periwinkles may be identified by the deep ridges in the shell (right).

Flat periwinkles do a superb impression of a bladder wrack gas bladder (above).

The larger common or edible periwinkle *Littorina littorea* will be familiar to many as a popular seaside-town snack; pickled winkles bring back childhood memories for me of family trips to Hastings on the south coast of England. The shell is shaped like that of land snail and is the largest British periwinkle. They are often found clustered together at low tide, awaiting the return of the tide. In contrast to flat periwinkles, females release fertilised eggs into the sea where they hatch into swimming larvae. Like the larvae of small periwinkles, they spend a few weeks floating among the plankton, before settling to the seabed and metamorphosing into the adult form.

The sturdy-looking common periwinkle (above) is the largest periwinkle of UK shores and tends to be gregarious (right).

Twirling top shells

Top shells you are likely to encounter on UK shores include the flat top shell *Gibbula umbilicalis,* grey top shell *Gibbula cineraria* and the toothed or thick top shell *Phorcus lineata*; all are grazers of the microscopic algal film and seaweed sporelings that coat intertidal rock with a slippery veneer. The grey top shell is also easily spotted grazing underwater on kelp fronds. These active little snails are often seen twirling around each other like colourful spinning tops. Close inspection reveals several fine tentacles around the rim of the shell that waft gently, scanning the water for information about their surroundings. It's worth consulting a seashore guide to learn the difference between each species and certainly a fun challenge for intermediate seashore explorers!

The thick or toothed top shell is the largest top shell (bottom left).

Grey top shell mowing a trail through the surface growth on a kelp frond (below).

The shell of flat top shell is quite obviously flattened and has striking patterns and colouration (top right).

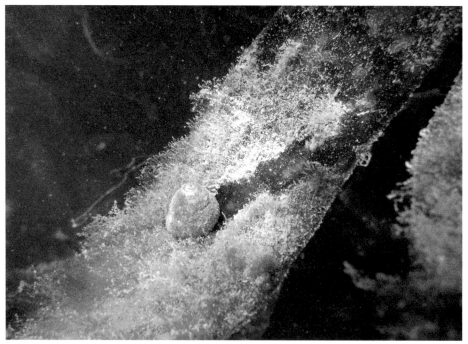

Carnivores

Boring snails

The dog whelk *Nucella lapillus* has evolved to exploit the rich supply of intertidal barnacles and mussels among which they are found. Their mouth and radula are borne on the end of an extensible siphon-like proboscis. Through a combination of rasping and chemical erosion by a corrosive secretion designed for the job, they wear a hole through the shell of their prey. The proboscis then secretes digestive enzymes through the hole, reducing soft tissue to a soup that is siphoned out as liquid nutrition. Boring the hole is a laborious process which can take up to five days to complete; not exactly fast food but clearly worth the effort.

Mussels have a defence against this particular attack. Living in large aggregations they glue themselves to rock or each other using strong, elastic threads called byssus. Once this remarkable adhesive has set it can neither be degraded nor deformed by water. For many years, biotechnologists have attempted to create artificial substances that rival this underwater adhesive, but the strength of

Dog whelk group on the shore.

mollusc-made glue remains superior. When under assault by a hungry dog whelk they begin to secrete more byssus, tethering their assailant to the sea bed for a slow death by starvation.

Eggs, eggs and more eggs

When it's time to breed, adult dog whelks gather together under sheltered over-hangs or in crevices in groups of thirty or more; some may call it an orgy, others a spawning aggregation. Either way, the eggs are fertilised and laid in vase-shaped protective capsules about the size of a barley grain that is cemented to the rock. Although each capsule may contain around 600 eggs, at least ninety percent of the eggs are unfertilised and function as 'nurse eggs' and are

Adult dog whelks grouped together among their eggs.

fed upon by the developing embryos. Hatchlings are fully-formed miniature versions of the adult and up to thirty well-fed individuals have been reported to emerge from a single capsule.

Sniffing siphons

Common whelks *Buccinum undatum*, the much larger relatives of dog whelks, actively sniff out sand-dwelling worms and carrion to feast on; they are found on sandy shores. Their tube-like siphon is extended upwards like an elephant's trunk, drawing oxygenated water over the gills for respiration. The siphon is also lined with chemoreceptors that allow the whelk to smell carrion in the water, directing them to the free

The mighty fine siphon of a common whelk in action.

buffet. These are most often found on sandy beaches at low tide, and regularly as empty shells washed up on the shore. Their spongy egg cases, known colloquially as sea-wash balls, are also found while beachcombing the strandline. Each ball is made up of many tiny capsules into which the eggs are laid; the whole mass is then stuck to a stone on the seabed. Hundreds of eggs are laid in each ball, yet few come to fruition; as with the dog-whelk eggs, most become food for the few that hatch first. Once detached from the seabed the empty case floats to the surface and is washed up on the shore for us to find.

The empty egg cases of a common whelk, known as sea wash balls, are often found by beach combers.

Dr Lou's low-down ...
The blue-rayed limpet's magical stripes

Recent research into the iridescent stripes of blue-rayed limpets has revealed their creation to be quite unique in the world of colour displays. Initial tests showed the lines to derive from below the surface of the shell and to be of structural origin. When the shell was sliced through and examined under a powerful microscope it showed distinct mineral layers arranged in an architecture that both reflected and absorbed light. The blue we see is a clever play on light created by the unique structure of the limpet's translucent shell. The precision lays in reflecting the exact blue required by the limpet and displaying it against a contrasting background so that it shines out. Combined with the curving pattern of the rays on the shell, the stripes can be clearly seen from all angles down to a water depth of twenty metres. So, what is the function of this scintillating splash of colour and who is it aimed at?

Blue-rayed limpet eyes are poorly developed and positioned beneath the shell, so the fanciful display is clearly not designed to impress fellow limpets. Combine this with the thinness of their colourful shells and flagrant positioning on the open plains of kelp fronds, means protection from predation is the only other explanation. They achieve this via Batesian mimicry, impersonating toxic or otherwise distasteful animals to ward off predators. The sea slug *Facelina auriculata* frequents the same habitats as the limpets and is often found among kelp. Although its overall appearance is very different, the iridescent blue stripes along its back warn predators of its toxic nature and could look similar to blue-rayed limpet stripes to the eyes of a predator. Perhaps the real reason is yet to be discovered; either way we have much to learn from this spectacular feat of evolutionary engineering.

Gem anemone partially covered in sand.

Sea Anemones

Sea anemones, along with corals, sea fans and sea pens, belong to a group of animals called Anthozoa – meaning 'flower animals' in Greek. Their brightly coloured fleshy blooms are a familiar sight at low tide and in rockpools when exploring our rocky coasts. Yet despite botanical references the sea anemones are fearsome animals with the ability to catch and subdue prey.

Flowers of the deep

In UK inshore waters there are about 40 species of sea anemone and more than 70 species of Anthozoa in total. They live in a diverse range of habitats from the brackish shallows of estuaries and the silty depths of sea lochs to intertidal rock, submerged shipwrecks and even some as parasites on the shells of other animals. Their variety of form and colour are truly dazzling. In this chapter I will throw light on these blossomed beauties by delving into the lives of a few species commonly encountered along UK coasts.

The Anthozoa have been around for a long time; their rich and diverse fossil record extending back at least 550 million years. When compared with all other animals, their body structure is rather simple in that they have fewer types of cells. In fact, they have fewer cell types than a single organ has in most other animals. Put simply, they are made up of just three tissue layers and are essentially laminar in construction, like three pieces of paper stacked one on top of the other. These two-dimensional layers are then folded origami-style, to yield a three-dimensional structure in the form of an anemone.

Each anemone is an elastic, muscular cylinder, open at one end and full of seawater; in fact seawater may account for eighty percent of its weight. The single opening to the outside world permits the entry of food into the central gastric cavity where digestion takes place. Any waste is then ejected from the same opening; mouth doubles as anus in the Anthozoan world.

The fact that they are mostly seawater means they change their shape and volume dramatically using muscular contractions and either opening or shutting the mouth. In water we see them with tentacles extended for feeding like flowers blooming in the sun; out of water they contract the tentacles becoming shiny beads on the rock or hanging loosely like deflated balloons. Anchoring them firmly to their preferred surface is a sucker-like pedal disc which provides a firm but non-permanent attachment. Although mostly sedentary when faced with predators, aggression from neighbouring anemones or inclement seasonal weather conditions, they are able to lift the disc and float away.

As well as being classic sit-and-wait predators, sea anemones are also supreme opportunists and will snack on any detritus drifting their way. In this way they minimise the energetic cost of obtaining food by waiting for it to come to them. Many are also able to absorb organic matter from the water column to supplement their diet. Most species tend to have a preferred diet which reflects both where they live and the size of their tentacles. The dahlia anemone *Urticina felina* for example lives squeezed into gullies close to or often on the seabed. They have thick robust tentacles that are heavily armoured with stinging cells and tend to feed on shrimps and small fish brought to them by surging waves. By comparison the plumose anemone *Metridium senile* likes to be elevated in the flow of the tide, attached to vertical walls and artificial structures such as pier pilings and wrecks. Their numerous fine tentacles are superbly suited to capturing plankton and small particles suspended in the water column.

Playing a central role in prey capture are the cnidae (meaning nettle cells) which respond to touch and chemical stimuli from their prey. Thousands of these cells are embedded in the surface of the tentacles. Although sea anemones are relatively simple animals in their overall construction, the cnidae are extremely complex and have attracted a lot of research interest over the years, especially for their potential in

The dahlia anemone has stout tentacles with a powerful sting to seize prey as it surges past in waves.

biomedical research. There are many different types of cnidae that serve different functions, but they are broadly categorised according to their structure. In sea anemones there are two types both of which discharge explosively on contact; spirocysts eject a sticky thread to hold struggling prey and nematocysts penetrate the prey like a tiny harpoon injecting toxin as they do so. The latter are responsible for the sting of both sea anemones and jellyfish.

The snakelocks anemone *Anemonia viridis* is one of the largest anemones found on UK shores with long mobile tentacles used to reach up into the water column and out across the seabed. Studies have shown that the snakelocks has twice as many entangling spirocysts than penetrating nematocysts in its tentacles, for holding and subduing its active prey as it is fed towards the mouth. By brushing your fingertips across the tentacles, you can experience the sticky sensation of the threads trying to hold the fingers, but you do not feel the sting of the harpoons due to the thickness of the skin there. They can however deliver a painful sting to other more sensitive parts of your body, as my husband found out by experimenting with his tongue. The result

was a surprisingly painful burning sensation that lingered on the tip for several days.

To supplement its diet of shrimps and other small invertebrates, the snakelocks anemone also gains energy from tiny, single celled algae called zooxanthellae that live embedded in its tissues. This is a mutually beneficial relationship where the anemone provides the algae with a protected environment and in return, the algae produce oxygen and recycle waste

Snakelocks anemone has two colour varieties – green with pink tentacles tips (top) and brown (bottom).

products from the anemone. Most importantly, the zooxanthellae supply the anemone with carbohydrates and amino acids produced by photosynthesis. Essentially, they function like tiny solar panels generating free energy from the sun for the anemone to use. In UK waters there are eight species of anemone that harbour zooxanthellae yet the nutritional benefits they bring are small compared to those enjoyed by their tropical relatives the reef-building corals. Here zooxanthellae produce up to 90% of the corals' nutritional needs, forming the basis of the second most bio-diverse and productive ecosystem on the planet. It is the ejection of the zooxanthellae from living coral that produces coral bleaching, a widespread global crisis caused by rising ocean temperatures. Coral bleaching is the greatest threat to the sustainability of coral reefs worldwide and is one of the greatest challenges scientists face in responding to the impact of global climate change.

Sea anemones reproduce in a variety of ways. Similar to other marine animals, many release eggs and sperm into the water. Once fertilised the eggs grow into larvae that swim in the plankton for a few weeks, whereafter they settle to the seabed becoming fully-formed adults.

Others employ much quicker, simpler tactics. For example, the gregarious plumose anemone *Metridium senile* found in deep water is able to create a new neighbour by tearing a small piece from the disc that attaches it to the seabed. This fragment then grows into a clone of the adult. The snakelocks anemone goes a step further, splitting itself in half length-ways in just a few days to double its numbers. The beadlet anemone *Actinia equina*, so familiar on UK rocky shores, are able to brood their offspring internally before ejecting the live young from the mouth, spitting them like grape pips to settle on the seabed. They are believed to be produced by a process of internal budding, where small fragments of the anemone tissue break off internally and grow into miniature replicas of the adult, though not all scientists agree on this.

Beadlet anemones are also known for their displays of aggression towards each other in competition for space on the rock. Each is well supplied with a battery of stinging cells in structures called acrorhagi that form blue knobbles at the base of the tentacles. In disputes the aggressor will lean over thrusting its acrorhagi into contact with its victim causing it to make a slow retreat. Other species such as daisy

Beadlet anemone with tentacles expanded ready for action surrounding the central mouth, a single opening that performs a double duty (top).

Beadlet anemone with tentacles retracted at low tide to conserve moisture (bottom).

anemone *Cereus pedunculatus* and plumose anemone have large inflatable catch tentacles which serve a similar offensive function.

With such a potent line of defence you might be surprised to learn that sea anemones have several natural predators. In fact, several species of sea slug feed exclusively on sea anemones. The shaggy looking aeolid sea slugs are a group of anemone connoisseurs that will gorge on whole anemones at a rate of three per week. They are distinguished from other types of sea slug by their possession of cerata; soft, horn-like outgrowths on their back containing specialised structures called cnidosacs. The cnidae are passed unharmed through the digestive system to cnidosacs (*cnido* from the Greek word meaning nettle) at the tips of the cerata. Here the cnidae are stored by the sea slug as second-hand weaponry for its own defence; we met one such sea slug *Facelina auriculata* on page 59, whose iridescent blue colouration warns of its potency and is thought to be mimicked by the blue-rayed limpet. Certain fish species also include anemones on their varied menu, nibbling at the tentacles or biting chunks from the disc rather than eating the whole thing. This is thought to allow the anemone to survive for subsequent visits. Perhaps the sting factor is

Acrorhagi (blue knobbles) may be used in aggressive disputes between neighbouring anemones.

only bearable in small mouthfuls; they must taste good to make it worth it.

Despite decades of study creatures as familiar and accessible as the beadlet anemone are still managing to perplex scientists with their curious methods of reproduction and intricately engineered stinging cells. Their flower-like appearance and sedentary habit belie a deadly microscopic armoury, aggressive outbursts toward neighbours and a penchant for self-replication. Beware the flowers of the deep, they are not what they seem.

Dr Lou's low-down ... Anemone biology in a nut shell

Offensive blue knobs – or acrorhagi (*ak-ro-ra'gee*) to give them their scientific name; these batteries of stinging cells are used in aggressive confrontations with neighbouring anemones.

Mouth-anus combo – anemones keep it simple with a single opening to the outside world that performs a double duty.

Sticky, stingy tentacles – a variety of complex, explosive cells that eject sticky threads and miniature harpoons ensure a nourishing fleshy meal is ensnared and directed towards the mouth.

Reproduction by self-mutilation – anemones can create their own party by tearing a piece off themselves or splitting in two.

Solar powered anemones – a few species have microscopic algae in their tissues that act like solar panels providing free energy from the sun.

Jellyfish thrive in the relatively warm, plankton-rich waters of midsummer.

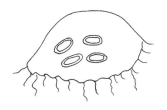

Sea Jellies

As the warmth of mid-summer settles over the land, coastal waters team with jellyfish and their wobbly relatives. In calmer bays and channels they may gather in the hundreds, clouding the water with their gently pulsating bells and trailing tentacles. Jellyfish are close relatives of sea anemones and corals; they are all classified in the Phylum Cnidaria (pronounced with a silent c) from the Greek word *knide*, which means nettle; members of the Cnidaria all share the unique ability to bear stinging cells that are used for both prey capture and defence. The broad structure of a jellyfish is fairly simple and consists of the umbrella-shaped bell from which the tentacles are suspended. They are 95% water that in the absence of bones provides a hydrostatic skeleton against which the swimming muscles act. The bell houses the gastric cavity and reproductive organs, with the mouth centrally placed to intercept food from the tentacles.

Turtle fodder

Jellies lack brains as we typically think of them; rather they have neurons organised into a nerve net that allow them to sense their environments, such as changes in water chemistry indicating food or the touch of another animal. The nerve net has some specialised structures located around the margins of the bell; statocysts provide balance and orientation and ocelli are sensitive to light. The traditional view of jellyfish as simple animals is being challenged with recent discoveries showing that this neural circuitry is in fact highly sophisticated. To add to this the stinging cells are extraordinarily fine-tuned, elaborate structures (as discussed in the *Sea Anemones* chapter) that have long juxtaposed with their otherwise primitive body plan. These are used to capture and subdue prey and for protection against predators. Despite this they have many known predators including fish, birds, shrimps, sea anemones, crabs and sea turtles. Due to their high water content they are not hugely nutritious, so for some they are a convenient supplement to their diet, while three of the seven species of sea turtles (leatherback, loggerhead and olive ridley) will happily gorge on jellyfish, biting off chunks or swallowing them down whole. Their approach is the all-you-can-eat buffet, and the leatherback turtle may put away in excess of 200 jellyfish in a day. In fact they swim thousands of miles each year, migrating from their breeding grounds in the Caribbean to feed on the jellyfish banquet on offer in our coastal waters. Their thick leathery skin is impenetrable to the stings, and the structure of their beak-like jaws allows them to grasp their slippery prey. They also have sharp, downward curving spines called papillae in their mouth and throat which help move the jelly to their stomach.

Wobbly transformers

The oldest ancestors of modern-day jellies lived at least 500 million years ago, and maybe as long as 700 million years ago. Their gelatinous form has survived all of the Earth's five major extinction events proving its resilience in the ocean environment. Their complex, phased life cycle certainly plays a big part in their success, allowing them to quickly take advantage of favourable environmental conditions. Throughout the life cycle jellyfish take on two forms, the medusa and the polyp. The medusa is what we think of as the adult jellyfish, a bell with tentacles hanging down that swims and stings; the polyp is the opposite, with the mouth and tentacles above, like a sea anemone. The medusa reproduces sexually, broadcasting sperm and eggs into the water. From the fertilised eggs hatch swimming larvae that spend a short time in the plankton before settling to the seabed and transforming into the polyp form. The polyp remains attached to the seabed and will complete the life cycle by cloning themselves; this involves budding off tiny, immature medusae called ephyrae that grow into adult jellyfish.

Quick guide to UK jellyfish

In UK waters we have five common species that are easily distinguishable; moon, compass, lion's mane, blue and barrel jellyfish plus a sixth rarer species called the mauve stinger that may be seen in deeper, oceanic waters. With the aid of this guide you can quickly identify your sightings of jellyfish and report them via the Marine Conservation Society website www.mcsuk.org or on the Big Jellyfish Hunt Facebook page.

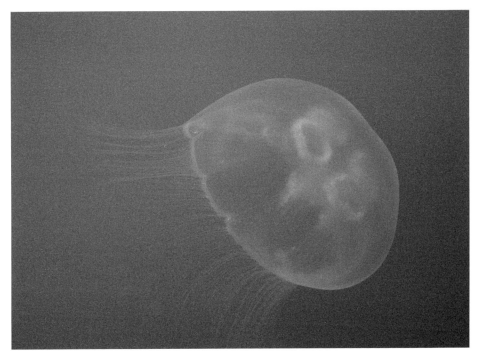

Moon jellyfish.

Compass jellyfish.

1. Moon jellyfish *Aurelia aurita*. Translucent and saucer-shaped with four distinct pink rings, the reproductive structures. They have four centrally placed tentacles and many short, fine tentacles around the margin of the bell that deliver a very mild sting. They are no cause for alarm while swimming.

2. Compass jellyfish *Chrysaora hysoscella*. Easily identified by dark brown, radiating lines on the bell that look like the points on a compass rose. Twenty-four slender tentacles hang from the margins of the bell while there are four thicker tentacles hanging centrally. The sting is moderately painful, much like a stinging nettle rash.

3. Lion's mane jellyfish *Cyanea capillata*. May grow large with a mass of shaggy brown tentacles centrally and many fine, long white tentacles along the margins of the bell that can reach thirty metres in length. The tentacles sweep the water column for prey like a fishing net. Approach this jellyfish with caution as the sting is rather potent.

4. Blue jellyfish *Cyanea lamarckii*. Bright blue, purple or pale-yellow colour with many fine tentacles; closely related to the lion's mane jellyfish though much smaller. The sting can be compared to that of a stinging nettle.

Lion's mane jellyfish (left).

Blue jellyfish (below).

5. Barrel jellyfish *Rhizostoma pulmo*. The largest jellyfish in the UK, up to one metre across the bell with eight central tentacles fused for much of their length to form a dense bunched mass. The structure bears hundreds of tiny mouth openings, each surrounded by miniature tentacles bearing stinging cells. The sting is harmless to humans and there are even reports of them being eaten by eighteenth century fishermen.

6. Mauve stinger *Pelagia noctiluca*. Small but striking in appearance, the bell is globe-shaped and covered with mauve warts that are packed with stinging cells. From the bell's margin hang eight stringy tentacles that may extend to three metres in length, and centrally dangle four thicker oral tentacles. It has an overall purple hue and may glow brightly at night with bioluminescence. Its Latin name translates as 'night light of the open sea'. Beware however, do not be lulled by its dazzling appearance; this jellyfish has a powerful sting that may illicit a severe reaction.

Barrel jellyfish (left).

Mauve stinger (below). Photo credit: Trevor Rees.

Rows of cilia on a comb jelly refract the light (right).

When is a jellyfish not a jellyfish?

The non-stinging floaters

Other transparent jellyfish-like creatures may also be seen floating in open water and though similar in appearance, are not true jellyfish. The most common are the comb jellies or cteno-phores (meaning comb bearers); each possesses eight rows of comb-like hairs or cilia along its body which beat to propel the comb jelly through the water. When these transparent combs catch the light, they produce an undulating rainbow effect that is quite mesmerising.

The comb jellies differ from jellyfish in two important ways. First, they do not possess sting-ing cells, but instead use specialised adhesive cells and mucous to trap plankton from the water column. Some, like the sea gooseberry

Pleurobrachia pileus, have long sticky tentacles that are extended to fish for planktonic prey, which are then reeled back towards the mouth where the catch is wiped off and swallowed. The larger comb jelly beroe *Beroe cucumis* lacks tentacles but makes up for it with a large mouth, gulping in prey that includes other comb jellies. The second major difference between jellyfish and comb jellies is in how they deal with waste, which was only discovered in 2015. When a true jellyfish finishes eating it just spits out any undigested waste; the same opening performs a double duty as we saw in sea anemones in the previous chapter. Comb jellies, on the other hand, have the luxury of a more graceful excretory option. Tiny pores near the rear end of the animal expel indigestible particles, for a more civilised in-one-end and out-the-other approach.

Colonial drifters

Another non-jellyfish floater that is seen year-round stranded on beaches and wafted along the sea surface is the by-the-wind sailor *Velella velella (*from the Latin *velum* meaning sail*)*. Delicate and transparent, they appear crafted from blown glass, yet they roam the world's oceans taken wherever the wind blows them.

They are made up of a bright blue, disc-shaped body supported by a thin and flexible floating plate, from which rises a thin diagonal crest that acts as a sail. The short feeding tentacles and reproductive components hang below the float. Though not true jellyfish either, they are closely related members of the Cnidaria called Hydrozoa; as with all cnidarians they possess stinging cells for capturing prey. Although each one looks like a single animal it is in fact a colony of animals living together with a shared purpose.

Less welcome as a visitor to our shores is another hydrozoan, the Portuguese man-o-war *Physalia physalis*. These pack the most potent sting of cnidarians in UK waters and are worth giving a very wide berth. With a translucent, gas filled float and bright blue stinging tentacles that can reach thirty metres long, they are impressive to behold. Like the by-the-wind sailor, each is a colony of hydrozoans made up of specialised individuals working together for the greater good. Studies have found that the gas-filled balloon may be trimmed like the sail on a boat; muscular contractions change both angle and shape of the float, the centre of buoyancy and degree of list allowing the man-o-war to actively alter its course.

Replacing fear with fascination

On a glorious summer's day, we pottered along the coast in our friend's new sailing boat to a spot we knew was good for swimming and freediving. As we anchored up and plopped over the side, we entered a scene that was teeming with pulsating sea jellies. Heading towards the rocks I was drawn towards a magical sea cave; as I entered the water grew calm and the light dimmed. At the furthest reach of the cave a blue jellyfish swam in circles then headed out for a beam of light illuminating the entrance. Realising that the cave had drawn me into its luminous depths to gift me a jellyfish, with grace I accepted, then inhaled deeply and sank into position to compose my shot. I remain truly grateful for the moment and an award-winning image that has been enjoyed by many (the front cover image).

---

1 *The sea gooseberry fishes for prey with its long, sticky tentacles.*

2 *With its sac-like body, beroe opens wide and engulfs prey whole.*

3 *Being at the mercy of the wind, by-the-wind sailors often end up blown on to shore.*

4 *Sightings of Portuguese man-o-war always cause a stir as their long blue tentacles carry a potent sting.*

Though jellyfish rouse fear in many people due to their tendency to sting, like every living organism on the planet they play a vital role in the rich web of life. Their other-worldly forms and quirky life stories add to the wonder of the natural world. Recent work on the juvenile ephyra of moon jellyfish discovered a phenomenon completely new to science, termed symmetrisation. Ephyra have a disc-shaped body with eight symmetrical arms. When researchers removed two arms from the jellyfish it rearranged its six remaining arms until they were evenly spaced around the body. Muscles in the jellyfish's body had pushed and pulled on the remaining arms until they were once again evenly spaced. Being able to heal by symmetrisation restores the symmetry crucial for jellyfish swimming and does so in a matter of days. Forms of self-repair observed in other groups of animals, such as regeneration of limbs, takes much longer. Jellyfish clearly have the edge when it comes to getting back on track.

Bloom and bust

Most sea jellies only live a few months before they die and disintegrate back to the ocean, while others may opt for a second chance at youth. When conditions are unfavourable, some species including compass, barrel, and moon jellyfish can reverse their development and effectively turn back into juvenile jellies to wait out the hard times. The young jellies (ephyra) are exceptionally hardy and can withstand months of starvation and may partly explain why many species of jellyfish can thrive in dirty, polluted, acidified, warm and oxygen-poor waters. In recent times, jelly blooms have been increasing in size and frequency worldwide, which has been interpreted as a troubling sign of a disturbed ocean ecosystem. Rising sea temperatures and overfishing have been cited as the causes in specific areas – this is certainly true in northern Benguela off the Namibian coast, where jellyfish biomass has now overtaken that of once-abundant fish stocks. Prey previously snaffled up by fish became available for the jellyfish, allowing them to thrive and proliferate and shift the ecosystem balance in their favour. Of growing concern is that as jellyfish populations swell there may be no natural control, and ecosystems may become jelly-dominated. Collectively jelly blooms have wreaked havoc on fish farms, caused widespread beach closures in the Mediterranean and prompted temporary shutdown of nuclear power operations owing to jelly-clogged intake pipes.

The role of sea jellies in ocean ecosystems is still being deciphered. The biggest challenge it seems is convincing those not enamoured by jellies that they are important and worthy of attention. Research is gaining momentum and is beginning to reveal their importance as both a food source and predator, and in transferring nutrients from one part of the ocean to another. Their longevity alone is a sign that we have much to learn from these ancient jellies of the sea.

Further reading

The secret lives of jellyfish, Gary Hamilton. Nature 531, 432–434 (24 March 2016)

Dr Lou's low-down ... Tagging barrels

Between 2008 and 2012 researchers from Swansea University and University College Cork in the collaborative EcoJel project fitted the first electronic tags to barrel jellyfish *Rhizostoma pulmo* in the Irish Sea. Every year huge blooms of tens of millions of jellyfish are recorded in this region. In an innovative bid to get a handle on the blooms, the tags allowed their movements to be tracked and swimming movement in relation to currents to be measured.

The results were fascinating and showed barrel jellyfish were able to actively change their swimming direction in response to current drift and changing current flows. This behaviour is key to the maintenance of blooms and reducing the probability of stranding and is necessitated by their weak swimming ability. Other creatures strong enough to out-swim the flow can set their desired course and adjust when they near their target with a burst of speed, while the barrel jellyfish must monitor the flow and make constant adjustments to remain on course. Such findings can help with predicting and managing blooms that may threaten bathing beaches, fish farms and other coastal industries.

The sand goby (this page), whale shark and pollack (overleaf) demonstrate the wonderful diversity of fishes.

Fishes

Sixty percent of all known species on earth with backbones are fishes, with more than thirty-three thousand species occurring worldwide. They are fantastically diverse, including species as different as the whale shark, pollack and sand goby.

Fish blueprint

Although each group has descended from entirely separate lineages, they have all evolved a general body plan suited to life in a dense medium that makes them superficially similar. Shared characteristics of the two main groups include streamlined bodies, gills for breathing, 'limbs' flattened into fins for swimming comprising two sets of paired fins, one or two dorsal fins, an anal fin and a tail fin. They also lay eggs, have jaws, skin that is usually covered in scales, and are ectothermic or 'cold-blooded' allowing their body temperature to vary with ambient temperature changes. The 'cold-blooded' description is a bit of a misnomer as their temperature will

The whale shark of tropical seas (left) and pollack (below) demonstrate the wonderful diversity of fishes.

The term 'fish' most precisely describes any animal with a skull and in most cases a backbone; that has gills throughout life and whose limbs, if any, are in the shape of fins.

For the most part they are divided between two major groups:

1. the cartilaginous fishes whose skeletons are made entirely of cartilage and include sharks, skates and rays;

2. the bony fishes whose skeletons are made of bone. These include most other fishes you could think of.

There is a third much smaller group of jawless fishes to which the hagfish and lampreys belong. They lack scales and have slippery, eel-like bodies, and instead of jaws have a round or slit-shaped mouth armed with horny teeth. Their skeleton consists of a simple rod of cartilage that runs the entire length of the body.

vary according to the water they are living in; they will only be cold-blooded if they happen to live in a cold place. As with any generalisation, each characteristic has exceptions – for example some fish lack scales and are naked, such as eels, while tuna, swordfish and some species of shark have the ability to generate their own body heat and are not reliant on external sources to raise their body temperature like other fishes. The fin arrangement often goes out the window too as we will see later on in this chapter with the ocean sunfish, whose tail fin and two sets of paired fins have been dispensed with altogether.

Eggs in or out?

Where reproduction is concerned, strategy also varies hugely with a spectrum of care that ranges from none at all – the spray-and-pray approach where eggs and sperm are released into the water in large quantities in the hope that at least some will survive to fruition – to nurturing of the eggs by the parents until hatching day. Often the male fish takes on the duty of guarding and raising the eggs. With all sharks the male and female will copulate; the males have reproductive structures called claspers that allow internal fertilisation of the eggs. In some shark and ray species the female retains them inside of her, giving birth to live young when they hatch, while with others the fertilised eggs are laid inside leathery egg capsules. All variations on the theme seem to be represented by the fishes making their reproduction a fascinating topic to ponder.

Sink, swim or float

Most bony fishes possess a swim bladder. Located in the body cavity, this gas-filled structure is used for buoyancy control, enabling the fish to maintain its depth without floating upward, sinking or swimming all the time. It also serves as a resonating space to produce or receive sound. In some bottom-dwelling and deep-sea bony fishes and in all cartilaginous fishes the swim bladder is absent, so that they sink when they stop swimming. Sharks have a large oily liver which is thought to compensate for the lack of a swim bladder.

Fish senses

Many fishes can see as clearly underwater as we can see in air, they can also hear, smell, taste and sense touch superbly well too.

Looks fishy

Perception of light underwater has required some unique adaptations in fishes because, as we learned in *Dr Lou's low-down … Light in the ocean* (page 40), light behaves very differently in air than it does water and diminishes with depth. These adaptations enable fish to see in lowlight conditions, murky water, and sometimes even over long distances. Most species have colour vision, some can see ultraviolet while others are sensitive to polarised light. Many deep-sea fishes have evolved super-power vision to pick up the faintest glimmers of light given off by other creatures. Studies have shown that the eyes and retinas of most fish provide good contrast detection, motion perception, and the ability to obtain a clearly focused image. In general, most fish are near-sighted, though some sharks are thought to be far-sighted.

The streamlined body form of fishes has done away with a neck and the ability to independently turn the head. As a result, the eyes usually protrude from the sides of the head, and each eye can move separately. The eyes can also rotate without moving the head, allowing vertical scanning of the surroundings and a horizontal view of almost 180 degrees. For some fish vision is less important than their other senses; many fish use their sense of smell or hearing to initially detect or find their food, and then use their eyesight to guide them on the final attack.

Smells fishy

Many fishes have an incredible sense of smell and their nostrils are dedicated solely to the purpose, leaving breathing to the gills. Bony fishes have their nostrils on the upper side of their head, while the cartilaginous sharks and rays have theirs on the lower side of their head. Each nostril is lined with layers of cells that are deeply folded into the olfactory rosette, a specialised area for scent detection; water is pumped in and out of the nostrils over the rosette for a continual flow of smells. The sensitivity of this smelling organ varies greatly among fishes and is truly impressive in some species;

the great white shark's legendary sense of smell allows it to detect small amounts of blood from an injured animal up to five kilometres away.

Where vision is unreliable in the murky underwater environment smell becomes particularly useful in identifying individuals of their own species, recognising specific places in their environment as with salmon returning to their spawning rivers, in reproduction, communicating danger to other fishes, and finding food.

Tastes fishy

Fishes sense of taste is well developed and is used mainly for food recognition. Taste buds in the mouth and throat, on their tongues and also on the outside of the body including lips, snout, fins and barbels (whiskers) have the ability to distinguish the difference between sweet, sour, salty and bitter. In this way they develop food preferences not only distinctive to species but also individuals.

Feels fishy

Fishes have an elaborate sense of touch through the lateral line system; a line of sensory cells running along the middle of the body from head to tail that perceive movement, vibration and

pressure gradients in the surrounding water. This provides spatial awareness and the ability to navigate in the environment and plays an essential role in orientation, predatory behaviour, defence, and social schooling. The direction and amount of movement made by prey can be detected from as far away as 250 metres in some species.

Sounds fishy

Sound travels five times faster in water than it does in air (which we will revisit in the *Cetaceans* chapter) enhancing communication to the extent that fishes have developed more ways of creating sound than any other group of animals with backbones. The options include grinding their teeth, rubbing bones together, stridulating their gill covers and expelling bubbles from their anuses. This has resulted in an impressive range of sounds including clicks, rumbles, chirps, pops and growls that has only recently been realised. Most sound production by fishes serves a social communication function and no more so than in the humble herring.

Sweet talking anuses – fish farts

Among the growing body of research on fish acoustics, herring (*Clupea harengus*) have been observed letting off a stream of air from their anuses accompanied by a high-pitched, repetitive popping sound. This is not the by-product-of-digestion sort of flatulence but a controlled expulsion of air from their swim bladder via the anus in order to message their shoal-members. Using farts each fish will talk to the rest of the shoal in order to maintain the precise grid formation of the shoal.

Ear ear

The lack of external ears in fish has no bearing on their ability to hear; their acoustic apparatus has developed internally as a series of bones called ostia that lie within the skull of the fish. The inner ear is sensitive to vibration rather than sound pressure, while the swim bladder acts as transducer that converts sound pressure waves to vibrations, allowing bony fish with a swim bladder to detect sound as well as vibration.

Sensitivity to noise and vibration differs among fish species, especially according to the anatomy of the swim bladder and its proximity to the inner ear. Species with no swim bladder (e.g. sharks) or a much reduced one (e.g. blennies) tend to have less sensitive hearing. In herring a gas duct connects the swim bladder to the hearing system, allowing them to pick up the sound of their fellow farters. Most fishes hear within the range of human hearing, but some species are sensitive to ultrasound and infrasound at the far ends of the sound spectrum that are well beyond the range of our hearing. Those with ultrasonic hearing are believed to have evolved this super-power hearing to tune into the high pitch sounds produced by their predatory dolphin foe. Herring release 60 short bursts of gas from the anal duct in around 6 seconds. The result is a single burst of high frequency sound that scientists have named Fast Repetitive Tick Sounds (FRTS). As this is beyond the range of hearing of most other fishes they are unable to detect the sound, but with their ultrasonic hearing herring can. The benefit is that herring are able to travel in huge shoals and remain relatively undetected by predators.

Fishes such as cod and plaice detect super-low frequency infrasound produced naturally by the large-scale movement of water around land masses. Scientists believe this background infrasound is used by the fishes for orientation during migration.

Fish sentience

For reasons that are not entirely obvious, we seem to have a lowly view of fishes compared to other animals. They are often referred to in terms of stocks as though their primary purpose is to feed us; cold-blooded even though they will take on whatever temperature their surroundings happen to be; unfeeling due to their fixed, expressionless faces and with limited brain function "*he's got a memory like a goldfish*". Yet like some moralistic clichéd tale, the more we learn about them the more it becomes apparent that our opinion needs to change. In the opening episode of the BBC's Blue Planet 2 series we meet Percy the orange-dotted tusk fish using a favoured coral anvil to smash open clams and hailed as the first example of tool use by a fish caught on film. Closer to home in UK waters, recent research has shown that shannies (small rockpool fishes) are able to form a mental map of their habitat, memorising prominent features for future navigation purposes. These observations are among a growing body of remarkable evidence that reveal fishes to be sentient, social, cunning and crafty. Their ability to experience fear, stress, playfulness, joy and curiosity makes them rather like us. I would like to advocate a fresh view on fishes, one of renewed respect and awe for these sensitive, conscious beings.

For this guide I have cherry-picked a selection of fishes you are most likely to come across in your coastal explorations of UK waters.

Bony fishes

Shanny: *Lipophrys pholis*

Mid-summer and a calm, clear sea invited me to snorkel at my favourite beach on the south coast of the St David's peninsula. I pulled on my wetsuit, gathered up my mask, fins and snorkel and trotted along the coast path and down to the water's edge. Squeezing on my fins my belly fluttered with excitement at what was to come. Shuffling into the shallows I flopped forwards and floated, and surveyed the glorious, sunlit vista before me. Sand eels darted across the bright sand in a tight sinuous shoal, each a mirrored shard that flashed in the

sunlight. Scattered rocks drew me over to their swaying stands of seaweeds, fluid and lithe in their synchronised movements with the ocean's vaguest swell. Gliding over rocks to the left I stopped to hover with my eyes a few centimetres from their walls. Familiar life forms spangled their surface; beadlet anemones bloomed crimson among barnacles, tentacles extended to intercept plankton. The barnacles fished too, their wispy legs extended to strain the rich sea-soup for sustenance. In my peripheral vision I spotted the snaky form of a shanny, a small familiar fish that turned to eye me with a flick and a wink. Its broad horizontal mouth and large round eyes give it a cheery, almost surprised expression. As I loomed in a little closer, it took off; I followed and as I caught up it settled to the rocks. Eyeing me again and still smiling, it took off once more; I accepted the invitation and followed on. I wondered where it was leading me as we repeated this merry chase several times when suddenly it grew tired of our flirtations and vanished among a swathe of serrated wrack. I was left feeling giddy with delight that I had entered the consciousness off this small fish and wondering what life was like for shanny.

Shannies, or common blennies as they are also known, are a widespread and abundant inhabitant of the shallow waters and rocky shores of our coasts. You may have glimpsed them darting for cover as you approach a rockpool or even tucked into a rock crevice at low tide, as they are able to breathe air when out of water. Growing up to sixteen centimetres in length and living for up to sixteen years they enjoy a long and apparently cheerful life; the wide mouth and high-set, independently rotating eyes and the habit of propping up on their pectoral fins gives them a happy, inquisitive expression. The speckled colouration of their smooth, scaleless bodies provides excellent

Shannies are well camouflaged on barnacle covered rock and can be approached with a little patience.

camouflage on the barnacle-covered rock they explore for food. With a varied, omnivorous diet they will snack on seaweed, as well as a range of small animals such as shrimps and worms, but they are especially partial to nipping off the limbs of feeding barnacles as they sweep out to catch plankton.

Thoughtful home-boys

During the breeding season (April to October in the UK) several hundred eggs are laid in a hole or crevice and guarded by the male shanny for a month or more until they hatch. At this time his colour darkens to almost black while the lips are a contrasting white. Recent research has revealed that male shannies show great fidelity to nest sites, much like migratory birds. After months of foraging offshore they will return to the same nest to breed and tend the

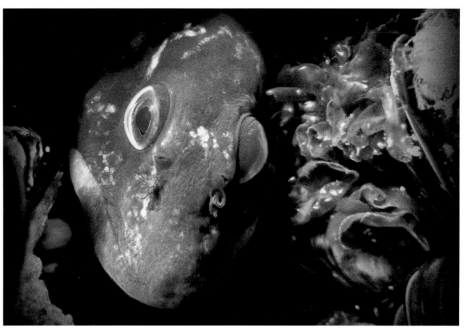

During the breeding season the male shanny darkens in colour and guards the eggs in his nest crevice.

eggs year after year. Learning the return route to familiar nest sites may save them energy in finding a new nest site and shows remarkable cognition not often acknowledged among fishes. Even in their day-to-day activities shannies exhibit homing behaviour, using the position of familiar landmarks on the seabed to navigate their way back to their home patch. That way they always know where there is a safe-haven when danger threatens and where to head for their next meal.

Ocean Sunfish: *Mola mola*

This peculiar grey, disc-shaped fish with rough skin (*Mola mola* means millstone) roams the world's tropical and temperate oceans in search of prey. Growing up to 3 metres long and 2.5 tonnes in weight this is the world's heaviest bony fish. This impressive heft is achieved on a diet mainly of jellyfish and scientists have observed them feeding solely on the most energy-rich gonads and arms, while leaving the less nutritious bell behind. Often described as a 'swimming head', it has no pelvic fins or tail fin and very tall dorsal and anal fins that beat in unison for swimming. The mouth is proportionally small and has fused teeth like a beak that is good for gripping its slippery prey. Most often sighted at the sea surface either sunbathing and drifting on their sides disc-like, or by the presence of their tall dorsal fin breaking the surface with a side-to-side motion; their appearance is unmistakeable.

Deep-diving sun worshippers

Recent tracking studies have revealed that during a typical day, sunfish will travel many kilometres a day and dive around 40 times to depths of 90 to 170 metres, although some have been recorded much deeper. The average deep dive for a sunfish lasts less than 10 minutes before they return to the warmer surface waters to warm up. This dependence on the sun to regulate their body temperature means that sunfish are only able to hunt in deep waters during the day. At night they simply rest and scavenge in the shallows. Short dives also serve as a searching strategy for the largest abundances of jellyfish, a behaviour exhibited by another jellyfish connoisseur the leatherback turtle.

Cleaners welcome

The skin of the ocean sunfish may carry more than 40 different types of parasites so periodically they will seek out cleaner fish to remove them. By adopting a non-threatening posture that is learned by both parties, they signal the cleaners to begin grooming. Individuals have even been reported at the surface encouraging sea birds to pick off parasites, a service that is crucial for maintaining health and vitality.

Eggs to spare

The ocean sunfish breeding strategy is of the spray-and-pray approach, releasing eggs and sperm into the water to mingle when other sunfish are nearby; a single female may broadcast 300 million eggs at a time to maximise the chances of a successful union. Such spawning events must be a cloudy affair and a feast for other marine animals. Those that survive hungry mouths grow into tiny larvae 2 millimetres in length that gather together in small schools for collective safety. Growth is rapid and they soon reach a size where they can brave it alone and begin their adult life of relative solitude, swimming the world's oceans gorging on jellyfish and sunbathing.

The ocean sunfish is unmistakeable with its disc-shaped body and long opposing fins. Photo credit: Lyndon Lomax.

Lesser weever fish: *Echiichthys vipera*

Spines in the sand

Though unlikely to be spotted (I've never seen one) the lesser weever fish is worth knowing about from a personal preservation point of view. Weever is derived from the Anglo-Saxon word for a viper as this fish can deliver a painful sting. The lesser weever likes warm water and will move into the shallows of intertidal sandy areas with the tide. During the day they are mostly inactive lying buried in the sand with just their eyes and dorsal fin exposed. When the weever is disturbed, strong spines on the gill covers and first dorsal fin are erected; on making contact venom is injected through spines into the unlucky assailant. The consequences of accidentally treading on or sitting on one is well-known at popular bathing beaches where it is a common summer occurrence. Thankfully soaking the affected part in hot water breaks down the venom and provides relief from the searing pain. Nocturnal bathers need not fear treading on the lesser weever, as they emerge from the sandy shallows at night to hunt shrimp, sand eels, gobies and other small bottom-living fish.

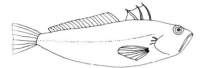

Sand eel

Seabird fodder

Sand eel is used here to refer to several different species in the sand lance family including the lesser sand eel *Ammodytes tobianus* and the greater sand eel *Hyperoplus lanceolatus*. All are distinctively slender with a pointed snout and

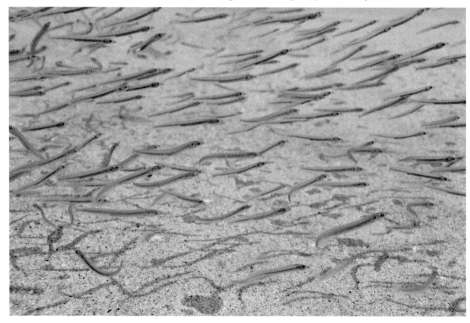

Sand eels form dense shoals in shallow water that change direction frequently to confuse predators.

protruding lower jaw, giving them an eel-like appearance. They swim in large, dense shoals close to the seabed and will burrow into the sand to escape predators. Spotted through the water as a swirling cluster of silver flashes they are a delight to behold. Sand eels feed on plankton and small bottom-living crustaceans and as shoaling fish have sociable lives. Yet their defining attribute seems to be as a major food source for many other fishes and seabirds. In fact, the breeding success of many UK seabird species such as puffins, terns and kittiwakes rely entirely on a healthy supply of sand eels. Research led by the Royal Society for the Protection of Birds (RSPB) suggested a link between the amount of sand eels caught by fishermen on the Dogger Bank in the North Sea and the breeding success of kittiwakes on Flamborough Head, Yorkshire. Higher intensity fishing lead to lower numbers of chicks being produced, highlighting a direct need to protect specific populations of sand eels from human exploitation for the sake of seabird conservation. Certainly a win for sand eels too, as their odds of survival versus a seabird, compared with a non-selective net cast around the whole shoal would be far higher.

Cartilaginous fishes

Basking shark: *Cetorhinus maximus*

Giant plankton strainers

The basking shark is the second largest fish on the planet (the whale shark holds first place) reaching an average size of 6–8 metres and just over 5 tonnes. The largest ever recorded was captured back in 1851 and measured more than 12 metres and 16 tonnes which is certainly as big as some present-day whale sharks; some individuals still rival this at 9–10 metres but are rare since commercial fishing decimated their numbers in the nineteen-hundreds. Sustained by a planktonic diet, they feed using well-developed gill rakers; these brush-like parts of the gills have evolved to strain particles from the water for filter feeding. By swimming along at around three kilometres per hour with their huge mouths agape, water is pushed through the gill rakers and out through the gill slits, leaving behind a delicious haul of zooplankton. This rich, soupy cocktail of shrimps, tiny fish, eggs and larvae sustains their huge size and they will travel to wherever it is most plentiful using their superior sense of taste and smell. Although they would appear to swim around filtering indiscriminately, researchers have found they do show a preference for a particular type of shrimp-like crustacean and will gather where these are most concentrated.

Friendly cruisers

Tagging of basking sharks has shown them to be highly migratory, swimming thousands of kilometres throughout the world's temperate oceans. During the summer months they are drawn to the plankton blooms of coastal waters and can be sighted all along the UK coast, with hot-spots around the Isle of Man, south-west England and the Hebrides in Scotland. Here they also gather to socialise with other basking sharks and mate. Schools of up to 100 individuals have been observed engaging in endearing social behaviour, with individuals swimming nose to tail in circles, yet little is known about their mating and reproduction habits. Exact figures are not known but researchers have estimated they give birth to fully developed live young every two to four years with a gestation period of between one and three years. Their life expectancy is around fifty years. After a summer of gorging on their favourite zooplankton and socialising, they move offshore for winter. Here they feed in deeper waters moving vertically up and down the water column consistent with the movement of zooplankton.

The large triangular fin of a basking shark cruising by.

Their appearance in UK waters is unmistakeable with their huge size and large triangular dorsal fin and slow swimming habit. Your first sighting can be a little unnerving as the large dorsal fin resembles that of a great white shark (Carcharodon carcharias) scything through the water. But their languid behaviour gives them away as they cruise along with their large mouths open, straining plankton. My first experience was while kayaking along the north coast of Skye in Scotland and then a few years later while circumnavigating Mingulay in the Outer Hebrides; each headland we rounded into a bay had its own basking shark straining the wild, plankton-rich waters. Part way through the journey we lost count of how many triangular fins coupled with the swaying tail fin and rounded nose breaking the surface we spotted. We had clearly found basking shark heaven.

Catsharks and rays

Mermaids' purses

Walk along the strandline of many beaches and you may find a mermaid's purse. These are the distinctive egg capsules of catsharks and rays. If it is pale brown and elongated with long tendrils on the corners it most likely housed the embryo of a small-spotted catshark (*Scyliorhinus canicula*) or a nursehound (*Scyliorhinus stellaris*). Both belong to a family of small sharks called catsharks that are often referred to as dogfish and are the only two species commonly found in UK waters. Identification of these egg capsules is fairly easy for this reason. The other type of mermaid's purse you may find has a squarer shape, is black rather than brown in colour and lacks tendrils, instead having short horns at each corner. This egg case may belong to one of several ray species and requires a more thorough approach to secure identification. The Shark Trust have produced a wonderful identification key to these egg cases and encourage explorers to report their finding to the Great Eggcase Hunt www.eggcase.org. The egg capsules are laid down by the females after mating who will swim in circles around a seaweed or other anchored structure to tether them by the tendrils. Each capsule contains a single embryo that develops into a miniature catshark and emerges after 7–9 months. The empty capsules often become detached and wash up on beaches for us to find.

The nursehound eggcase is often found washed up in the strandline and easy recognisable by its elongated shape, brown colouration and wiry tendrils (right).

Skate or ray egg cases are square-shaped and have short horns at each corner (below).

The egg case of the small-spotted catshark is similar to that of the nursehound but smaller and less robust looking (bottom left).

Sharky magnetism

Once the tiny shark leaves the leathery confines of its egg capsule it must learn to forage for food. Catsharks hunt at night, eating a wide range of prey that includes bottom-living fish, crabs, sea snails and worms buried in the seabed. As with other fishes, catsharks have a remarkable sense of smell and acute hearing for detecting prey, but they also use electroreception to pick up weak electrical fields produced by other living animals. Peculiar to sharks and rays, small clusters of electrically sensitive receptor cells positioned under the skin in the head called ampullae of Lorenzini allow them to sense prey hidden beneath the sand or in nearby crevices. Though only operational at close-quarters it adds another dimension to an already impressive repertoire of senses that make sharks formidable predators. In addition to the weak electric fields produced by their prey, the ampullae of Lorenzini are also able to detect the Earth's electromagnetic field, throwing light on the homing and migration abilities of sharks.

With SCUBA and advances in underwater camera equipment, tagging technologies and improvements in underwater sound-recording

The ampullae of Lorenzini are visible as black pores on the head of this whale shark that occurs in tropical seas and are unique to the cartiliginous group of fishes.

technologies researchers are uncovering aspects of fish behaviour that would have seemed like fantasy a generation ago. It seems the more we learn about our oceans and the creatures that live there the more we realise how mistaken our assumptions have been. We share so many traits with so many other life forms; if rockpool fish can use their small brains to cooperate, innovate, show virtue and express emotion, surely we can use our large brains to do the same for our imperilled oceans.

Dr Lou's low-down ... Sharky constellations

In his book *What a Fish Knows* Jonathan Bolcombe attests that *"It is a fact of biology that every fish, like the proverbial grain of sand, is one of a kind,"* and that *"Each fish is a unique individual, not just with a biology, but with a biography."*

Aside from emerging evidence that individual consciousness exists in fishes, individuals of certain species can be recognised from distinctive patterns on their skin. Whale sharks, the tropical relatives of our native basking sharks, are the largest living fishes reaching more than 12 metres in length and 14 tonnes in weight and are long lived with a life span between 60 and 130 years. Their skin is marked with a mesmerising pattern of pale spots and stripes that is unique to each shark. Researchers worldwide now use a modified NASA algorithm, a pattern recognition formula designed to examine star constellations, to analyse the distinctive spot patterns of whale sharks. Like human fingerprints, no two whale sharks have the same pattern, so by photographing the left flank just behind the gills of individual sharks, each sighting can be compared to the worldwide online database 'Wild Book for Whale Sharks' www.whaleshark.org. In this way movements of individuals can be tracked, and the information used to steer international conservation measures for these highly migratory sharks. Similar photographic databases also exist for manta rays and leopard groupers that also show unique individual skin patterns.

Flexible webbed feet make good swimming paddles.

Seabirds

Seabirds spend most of their lives at sea and have developed a range of characteristics that allow them to flourish in this environment. Webbed feet, salt glands, modified wing shape, waterproof feathers, plumage colouration and bill shape all benefit the seafaring lifestyle. Most seabirds have flexible webbed feet that enable them to swim efficiently and act as propellers when taking flight. For seabird purists, they are placed far back on the body in a position that maximises paddling efficiency. This comes at a cost of being poorly placed for walking on land, a worthy trade-off when you spend most of your time at sea.

Specialised salt nasal glands are found in many seabirds just above the eyes. These glands desalinate sea water enabling them to enjoy an internal drink of fresh water, while the salt is then secreted from their nostrils. The wing shapes of seabirds are adapted to their feeding and flying habits. Some seabirds, like the Arctic tern *Sterna paradisaea* which migrates from pole to pole every year, have long and tapered wings that are essential for covering long distances with minimal effort. Other species such as the puffin *Fratercula arctica* have short and sturdy wings, which allow them more control when diving underwater for feeding. Compared to their inland relatives, some seabirds have developed waterproof feathers that help them with buoyancy and add extra insulation.

The countershading of plumage (dark on the top, light on the bottom) found in many seabirds serves as camouflage, especially in smaller birds. The darker plumage above provides them with protection from aerial predators, while the white plumage below ensures that they are not seen from below the water against the bright under surface of the sea.

Seabirds have also been found to have more feathers relative to their body size than their land counterparts as an adaptation to the colder temperatures of an aquatic lifestyle. Adapted bill shapes are seen in many seabirds and none more impressive than the northern gannet whose aerodynamic bill spears through the water as it plunges after fish. Others, like the puffin, have developed serrations inside the bill that secure fish while they open their mouths to catch more. This enables them to rack up multiple fish on a single fishing trip; the average catch is around ten fish per trip but the record in Britain is a whopping sixty-two fish.

With such a varied collection of wondrous birds I've selected a few of my favourites from those you are most likely to encounter while exploring the coast in UK waters.

Puffins have short wings that are ideal for swimming underwater and give them their characteristic whirring flight.

Common guillemot

"I am a guillemot,
I use my bill a lot
I get the fish out of the wet
I get my fill a lot.
I live on ledges
Vertical edges
Eating-wise, I do not know what veg is …"
    Excerpt from 'Guillemot' by John Hegley

Four black and white birds with pointy beaks
bob a few metres from the bow of my sea kayak.
Each one dips its head in the water a few times
in quick succession, perusing the scene below.
Then quite suddenly, as if something caught its
eye, the first up-ends itself and with a flick of the
tail slips beneath the surface; a second bird fol-
lows suit, then after what seems like a moment
to synchronise, the last two dive together. With
wings partly folded they row to the depth's
penguin-like and quickly vanish from sight.
Tiny ripples mark where they once sat, and I
feel a pang of admiration and longing in my
chest to plunge after them; oh to be a guillemot.

Guillemot floating at the surface between dives.

Guillemots belong to a family of birds called auks that also includes murres, auklets, puffins and murrelets. They share the ability to 'fly' underwater as well as they can through the air. The common guillemot (*Uria aalge*) is the most abundant auk in the British Isles and like most seabirds only comes to land to nest and rear the young, which it does gathered together in great rowdy colonies on steep, inaccessible sea cliffs. The rest of its life is spent at sea, swimming and hunting the depths for its diet of small fish, squid and crustaceans. After 40 years studying the common guillemot on Skomer Island Tim Birkhead suggested in his book *Bird Sense* that guillemots share many similarities with humans "*they are extremely social, forming friendships with their neighbours, and occasionally helping them with childcare; they are*

monogamous (albeit with the occasional fling); male and female pair members work together to rear offspring, and pairs sometimes remain together for as long as 20 years."

In addition to decades of field observations, modern technology is helping to reveal remarkable details about their lives beyond the breeding colonies; scientists have become guillemot voyeurs, tracking their diving and travelling habits from land to sea and back.

Wonky eggs

Life begins for a guillemot as a pear-shaped egg laid directly on to bare ledges of steep coastal cliffs, in colonies that can number several thousand. The eggs protruded shape is significant for survival as when it is knocked by the careless foot of a neighbouring bird, it simply pirouettes instead of rolling off. With breeding densities of up to 70 pairs occupying a single square metre this is a very real hazard and is a beautiful example of natural engineering in action.

Love thy neighbour

Being in constant bodily contact with one's neighbours may be a little stressful at times but such densities are key to their breeding success;

a tightly packed battalion of guillemot beaks can protect eggs and chicks from predatory gull and raven attacks. Proof of it's worth is provided by the return of each pair to the same tiny patch of rock year after year. With just a few centimetres square to call their own they get to know their neighbours rather well. Lasting friendships are formed as they stand there incubating the eggs on their fleshy feet. Such trust is crucial once the chicks hatch; in general parents take it in turns to bring fish back to feed their hungry offspring but on occasion both parents may head to sea to forage leaving the chicks under the supervision of their neighbourhood crew.

Denizens of the deep

When it comes to fishing, guillemots demonstrate superb underwater skills. They dive to great depths on a single breath of air in pursuit of a meal and do so repeatedly with only short rests to replenish oxygen supplies before diving again. Typically, they dive to depths of 30–60 metres but have been recorded at 180 metres. The Brünnichs guillemot (*Uria lomvia*), a close northern relative of the common guillemot, holds the record for the deepest dive for a flying bird recorded at 210 metres, while the emperor penguin takes the crown for deepest diving bird having been clocked foraging at 500 metres. Impressive statistics indeed that dedicated human free divers have come to rival; the current world record for deepest dive on a single breath of air is 214 metres held by Herbert Nitsch, 'the deepest man on Earth'. The technique to achieve this though allows for use of a weighted sled to descend and an air-filled balloon to return to the surface. Not quite how guillemots play the game but a mighty achievement all the same.

For the feathered submariners their depth pursuits are for food and not records – they follow their prey to the deep in order to feed

Guillemots are neighbourly birds and form lasting friendships within breeding colonies.

Guillemots pursue fish underwater to depths of up to 180 metres.

themselves and their hungry chicks. Their preferred food is small schooling fish such as sand eels, capelin and sprats pursued in a high-speed chase. Once caught a single fish is carried head first so that the tail droops from the end of the beak.

Voice recognition

On returning to the colony delivery is the next challenge – how to relocate their chick among the hordes of other young guillemots? With so many birds crowded together life in the colonies is a noisy affair with parents calling to chicks and each other at regular intervals. Both chick and parents are able to distinguish each other's calls from the din of the crowd which they learn while the chick is still inside the egg.

To achieve this, they have adapted a hearing system that allows them to filter out the call from all the background noise and is termed the cocktail-party effect. Not only is this important for maintaining contact in such a dense colony but is vital when the time comes for the young guillemots to begin life at sea. At three weeks of age and under the cover of dusk, the chicks launch themselves en masse over the cliff edge towards the sea. Having not yet developed their flying feathers they face a perilous plummet to join their fathers waiting on the water below. Reunited via their individual calls they remain together for several weeks with fathers tending the chicks until they have honed the skills to fish for themselves.

In-bird GPS

Once the chick has fledged parents and chicks go their separate ways and head to sea for the winter. During recent years, electronic miniaturisation has allowed tiny geolocators to be attached to the legs of these birds that have revealed some surprising travel itineraries. In the course of a year guillemots nesting on Skomer Island fly south to the Bay of Biscay for a few weeks then travel 1,500 kilometres north to spend much of the winter off north-west Scotland, then back to Bay of Biscay again in the few weeks before the breeding season, and finally back to Skomer Island. With only the oceanic horizon for reference this begs the question, how do they navigate? Like other birds they possess a magnetic sense, a compass that allows them to read directions from the earth's magnetic field. They also possess a magnetic map that allows them to identify their location – a living version of GPS that human explorers can only dream of.

The guillemot story is a revelation, a beautiful tale of deep-diving, faithful and compassionate birds that form friendships and can navigate oceans without a map. But what more could future technologies reveal about life as a guillemot? Perhaps a sequel will unfold in years to come but we'll have to wait and see ... as a guillemot, I am not.

Oystercatcher

A loose group of birds browse on a small island of rock on a rising tide; their black and white plumage and startling crimson beak stand out from the dark background and identify them as oyster catchers. Swell surges at the rock, rising up the legs of one bird, sometimes reaching its belly. It pipes in protest and flaps up and onto a dry rock, shaking out its feathers in displeasure. It is searching for limpets that have released their tight grip on the rock to graze as the tide returns. The slightest gap between the shell's rim and rock will allow the oyster catcher purchase to prize it off. Once off it is flipped upside down and the juicy flesh plucked from the shell; a mussel may be similarly dispensed with, as the bill tip is thrust between the two shell halves and the strong muscle that clamps them shut is sliced with a deft jab of the chisel-like beak. Alternatively, they may hammer on the shell, cracking it open with brute force. I watch as two birds march around the shore testing limpet shells, occasionally going to work on one. These two are clearly shellfish specialists with an opportunistic streak as I see one carry off something long and thin and wriggly – most likely a blenny, a common rockpool fish.

Hammer, chisel or tweezer beak?

Numerous elegant studies of the oystercatcher *Haematopus ostralegus* show that the bill becomes shaped according to their feeding behaviour. 'Stabbers' and 'chiselers' have laterally compressed bill tips, while 'hammerers' have a distinctly blunt bill tip; each characteristic is created by the abrasive action of handling the hard shells of their prey. Others have a preference for worms over shellfish and have pointed, tweezer-like bill tips refined by the even wear of probing into sand or mud. Diet preference thus results in a bill shape that is wonderfully suited to securing a successful meal. Oystercatchers seen working limpets on the shore will have honed both skills and bills with practice, yet they remain flexible if the need dictates. Their bills are uniquely specialised for coping with wear and grow at an impressive 0.4 millimetres per day, which is three times faster than human finger nails grow. Such swift growth means that the bill can change shape rapidly to suit feeding style, allowing them to switch from worm-eaters to shellfish hammerers to stabbers, and back again through the course of their long lives. Like many seabirds, oystercatchers are renowned for their longevity and may live as long as forty years, so it pays to be flexible in a changing world.

The pied plumage and crimson beak of the oyster catcher is unmistakeable (top).

Evidence of a limpet feast by a shell-fish specialist oystercatcher (bottom).

Flying sea pies

By now you may be wondering how they got the name oystercatcher when no mention of oysters has been made. Their modern name is thought to be an eighteenth-century Americanism as their New World counterpart the black oystercatcher does in fact feed mainly on oysters. Before this name became familiar they were called sea pies locally, referring to their pied plumage. Pioden fôr is the name by which they are known in Welsh. Next time you're at the coast keep your eyes open for these flying sea pies.

Manx shearwaters are beautifully engineered for long-distance flight. Photo credit: Dave Boyle.

Manx Shearwater

The islands of Skomer and Skokholm host around 165,000 breeding pairs of Manx shearwaters *Puffinus puffinus* during the breeding season – some fifty percent of the UK population and the largest known concentration of this species in the world. Every year they migrate thousands of miles from their breeding burrows on the offshore islands of Pembrokeshire to their winter residences off the coasts of southern Brazil and Argentina. They are superbly adapted for these long-haul flights, with long narrow wings that are made for gliding and shearing over the water. The lack of ground predators on the offshore islands mean they are safe to nest in burrows, though they still return under the cover of darkness to avoid predatory gulls.

Burrowing birds

Between early and mid-May a single egg is laid in a burrow excavated by the parents. They take turns to incubate the egg, each doing from four to eight days at a time while the other goes off to sea to feed. The incubation period is one of the longest of all birds; the adults spend around fifty days sitting on the egg deep inside the nest burrow, before the chick hatches into the world towards the end of June. The chick will then spend another seventy days ensconced, being fed by its parents before its maiden flight to the open sea.

Mighty migrations: fly me to the moon

The parents leave the chick towards the end of August and head south to South America, a journey of more than six thousand miles; ringing studies have shown that some birds cover the distance in less than a fortnight. Fledgling Manx shearwaters head off to sea at night, without their parents, and immediately head for South America; a truly epic journey for their first flight and begs the question, how do they know what to do and where to go? Similar to the guillemot, it is believed they are able to see the Earth's magnetic field and are guided by their internal compass. Once its webbed feet lift off from the cliffs of Skomer Island, it will then spend the rest of its life at sea only returning to land for brief periods to breed. For a young shearwater it may be seven years before it feels solid earth again. Manx shearwaters are among the longest-lived birds in the world with ringing studies showing one individual reaching fifty-five years of age. During their long life-time of epic migrations they will cover a distance equivalent to ten times to the moon and back.

Though built for extended periods of flight with long, stiff wings they are surprisingly agile underwater too. The webbed feet provide most of the propulsion, but they will also beat the partially folded wings to add speed and can dive to a depth of over fifty metres in pursuit of prey. Several feeding behaviours are observed, which include flying dives, surface sighting and seizing, duck dives, short dives and prolonged foraging dives. They are highly manoeuvrable underwater and capable of changing direction with ease.

Fulmar

Seabird super-snout

The seafaring fulmar *Fulmarus glacialis* is built for long-distance cruising much like the Manx shearwater; in fact, they both belong to the group of birds referred to collectively as tube noses that includes albatrosses, fulmars, shearwaters and petrels. At close quarters the tubular nostrils set on top of the bill are prominent, giving a heavy look to the bill. Tube-nosed seabirds have a superb sense of smell and can detect food items from many kilometres away. They will track across the wind until they find a scent and then follow it upwind to its origin.

Feeding at the surface they will bob underwater to forage on a variety of prey that includes fish, small squid, shrimp, krill and marine worms; they will also scavenge on carrion and fish offal discarded by fishing fleets.

Fulmars are highly pelagic outside the breeding season and are strong fliers, with a stiff wing action quite unlike the gulls, thus enabling them to glide for efficient long-distance flight. Spending all their time at sea means they never drink freshwater, relying on the desalination plant in their noses to remove the salt from seawater ingested with their food.

Cliff crooners

Like other seabirds they return to land only to breed and raise their chicks. They are a little clumsy while walking, squatting on their lower legs with a waddling gait. Courtship takes place on cliff edges and offshore rock pillars, where the pair cackle and croon at one another; a single egg is then laid on any convenient depression which may be lined with plant material. Incubation is long and takes around fifty days with the parents sharing the task in shifts. Once the chick hatches, they feed it with a fish paste regurgitated from their stomachs.

Fulmar nesting high on a cliff edge.

Foul defence

Both parents and chicks are notorious for their potent self-defence mechanism while on the nest, whereby a stinky, waxy oil (described as "malodorous volatiles" in scientific literature) is squirted from the mouth towards intruders. The consistency is such that it cannot be cleaned from the feathers or fur; a potentially fatal outcome for any predator if their flight feathers or insulating fur is compromised. In fact, the name Fulmar is derived from the Old Norse word fúll meaning foul, and már meaning gull.

Gannet

As I arrive at the tidal headland of St David's Head, I spot a cloud of gannets circling over the water, eyes down-cast, searching for fishy silhouettes. Like smoke above fire, they herald fish and fellow hunters beneath the water, so I check the surface for signs of harbour porpoise too, the rise of a fin and a smooth dark back. Sure enough, a small group of porpoises burst into view, feasting on the fish brought there by the tide. It's not long before the gannets plunge among the porpoise, launching their aerial attack. When they begin the plummet, the wings bend and stiffen, until the split second the beak touches the water; at this moment the wings are hinged up and back as though lopped off at the body, and the bird morphs into a torpedo. In this way their streamlined form penetrates deep underwater allowing them to seize fish far below. As they arrow into the water and vanish, white columns of bubbles begin to rise from which the gannets are fired back to the surface looking crumpled and untidy. They shake themselves back to order with the fishy prize discernible as a bulge in the throat. It's quite a show and happens in quick succession, as one bird after another slips in and bobs back up.

Torpedo birds

Gannets *Morus bassanus* are the largest sea-birds in the north Atlantic, having a wingspan of up to two metres. They have bright white plumage with yellowish heads, black-tipped wings and long powerful bills. Gannets hunt fish by plunge diving into the sea from a height and pursuing their prey underwater. Dive heights vary according to the depth at which their chosen fish lurks; spectacular plunges may occur from a height of up to thirty metres, achieving speeds of 100 kilometres per hour as they strike the water, enabling them to catch fish much deeper than most airborne birds. Once underwater they may continue the pursuit, using their strong pectoral muscles to swim with bent wings down to depths of up to ten metres. Such a specialised, high impact lifestyle requires some structural adaptations to give them the edge and preserve their longevity. To prevent high speed irrigation of their airways, they lack external nostrils, instead these are located inside the mouth. They also have air sacs beneath the skin on the face and chest, to cushion the impact and act like emergency air bags in a car. With eyes positioned far forwards on the face, their superior binocular vision allows them to judge distances accurately; a circling gannet can pinpoint fish from a height of thirty metres, on foggy days and through murky water.

Gannets have a wing span of up to 2 metres and plunge dive for fish.

Fencing, noisy neighbours

Gannets breed in huge, dense, extremely raucous colonies called gannetries, on islands, cliffs and stacks. Pairs usually bond for life, and both mates participate in all aspects of parental care. They have a rich repertoire of behaviours including a greeting ceremony between pairs, known as 'mutual fencing'; a bowing display vital for maintaining territory within the colony and sky pointing which indicates intention to take flight. The nests are evenly spaced on sloping rock or wide ledges, their guide being pecking distance; the gannet bill is strong and spear-like and used aggressively as a weapon against unwanted neighbourly attention. Seaweeds and other plants, and materials such as feathers are heaped up to form the nest into which the female lays a single, chalky egg.

Unlike many other birds, gannets do not have a brood patch, so their overlapping webbed feet are used to incubate the egg for around forty days. Once fledged, it takes five years for gannets to reach maturity; first-year birds are completely black, and subsequent sub-adult plumages show increasing amounts of white.

With about two thirds of the world's population, the UK is the most important nesting ground for northern gannets. They live mainly in Scotland, including the Shetland Islands and Bass Rock in the Firth of Forth; they also nest on Bempton Cliffs in Yorkshire, Grassholm Island, Pembrokeshire and Alderney in the Channel Islands.

Gannetry on Grassholm island, Pembrokeshire.

Shag

Every cormorant is a potential shag

The shag *Phalacrocorax aristotelis* is one of two species of the cormorant family found in the UK, the other being the cormorant. They can be tricky to tell apart, especially in the case of young birds but a few features to look out for are:

Shag

Smaller and thinner than the cormorant with a more rounded head and delicate beak. Neck straighter in flight. Adult breeding plumage is black with green glossy sheen and wings tinged purple. Prominent black head crest. Young birds are dark brown above, pale brown below and sometimes show the hint of the adult head crest.

Shag on the nest in breeding plumage.

Cormorant

Stouter, more powerful beak than the shag. Neck thick and kinked in flight. More extensive yellow skin around the mouth and white cheeks. Adult breeding plumage is similar to shag but with a white thigh patch.

Shags are present year-round along UK coasts.

Fishy pursuits

With all four toes on each foot being webbed, shags are well equipped with powerful paddles for swimming and pursuing fish underwater. At the surface they swim with the body low and bill raised and dive with a characteristic leap to swim underwater. They may remain submerged for several minutes, diving to depths of more than 45 metres. They eat a varied fish diet foraged from the sea bed, but their preference is sand eel; these shoaling fish are lightning fast underwater yet are preyed upon by many seabird species. Larger prey is often brought to the surface and swallowed head-first.

Soggy feathers

Emerging from the water shags are often seen perching on rocks with their wings outstretched to dry as their feathers are not waterproof like other aquatic birds. They breed in loose colonies on coastal cliffs making a nest of heaped-up vegetation in a crevice, small cave or beneath overhangs. Unlike other true seabirds that head out to sea once breeding is complete, shags will over-winter along the coast and can be seen year-round.

Dr Lou's low-down ... Seabird voyeurs: high-tech tracking

Speculation around where seabirds go once they disappear from land has existed for many years; unveiling the mystery has become increasingly important in recent years, with severe declines in seabird numbers. Clues that these declines are related to a lack of safe and plentiful feeding opportunities have led scientists to embrace improvements in technology to help solve these mysteries. Advances in the miniaturisation and mass-production of high-precision GPS tags has enabled the detailed movements of large numbers of seabirds to be tracked, including the UK's smallest breeding seabird the storm petrel. These tiny birds are little bigger than a sparrow, weigh in at 30 grams and have recently been tracked feeding off the west coast of Ireland with devices weighing just a few grams.

Since 2010 the Royal Society for the Protection of Birds (RSPB) and collaborating scientists have tracked more than 2,000 seabirds of twelve species from nearly forty colonies around the coasts of Britain and Ireland. This has shown that some birds travel much further from their breeding colonies than previously thought; razorbills and guillemots nesting on Fair Isle, Shetland regularly travel more than 300 kilometres in search of food for their young, bringing them into potential conflict with marine developments previously thought to be well beyond their range.

Gannets fitted with satellite tags at Bempton Cliffs, Yorkshire travel to important feeding areas between 50 and 150 kilometres from the colony. These feeding grounds overlap with areas proposed for offshore wind farms, including the Hornsea zone, which is closest to Bempton Cliffs. After breeding, the birds roamed in various directions; some remained in the southern North Sea, for at least a few weeks while others started their southward migration, reaching north-west Africa before the end of October or migrated north, around the north of Scotland, before continuing south into the Bay of Biscay.

Various tag technologies have been deployed including combined video tag and GPS such as 'Gannetcam', underwater dive loggers, accelerometers, remote download GPS tags and 'texting tags' which send seabird location data by text message. Such technology is now providing vital information for effective conservation of the marine environment.

The Phocidae have no external ear flaps and hairy flippers as seen on this Atlantic grey seal, UK.

Seals

Seals belong to the group of animals called pinnipeds (fin-footed) that includes thirty-four species of aquatic, carnivorous mammals. The pinniped group is sub-divided into three families; true seals (Phocidae), eared seals (Otariidae) and the walrus (Odobenidae) and each show defining characters. The true seals are those with backward facing hind flippers and relatively small fore flippers, and include the familiar Atlantic grey seal of UK shores. Progress on the land is laborious as they haul along with their fore flippers, yet in the water they are transformed, swimming swiftly with powerful side thrusts of the hind flippers. All of the Phocidae lack external ear flaps and have hair covered flippers. The eared seals include fur seals and sea lions and are able to walk on land with their forward-facing hind flippers and large fore flippers. They are extremely agile in the water and swim by sculling with their powerful fore flippers. The Otariidae have small external ears and their flippers are hairless. The walrus is the sole member of the Odobenidae and although it looks a little like a sea lion with forward-facing hind flippers, it moves rather awkwardly on land, lacks external ears, and has long tusks and mostly hairless skin.

The Otariidae have small external ears and hairless flippers as seen on this California sea lion Zalophus californianus in Baja California Sur, Mexico (left).

Harbour seal (above).

Pinnipeds are found from the poles to the tropics, but most inhabit the cold waters of the northern and southern hemispheres; roughly a quarter of the 34 species live permanently in tropical waters. The world's most abundant seal by a long shot is the Crab eater *Lobodon carcinophagus*; it is a true seal widely distributed through Antarctica with an estimated population of at least 7 million and possibly as many as 75 million individuals. Their success is attributed to specialised feeding on the super-abundant Antarctic krill and not crabs as their name might suggest. In contrast, the Mediterranean monk seal *Monachus monachus* is the world's most endangered seal; once abundant, it has disappeared from most of its former range and in 1985 was declared by the International Union for Conservation of Nature (IUCN) to be among the twelve most endangered species worldwide. Conservation measures introduced over the last 30 years have helped to stem the decline, and there is now evidence of recent small increases in all known subpopulations.

Female seals are referred to as cows, males as bulls and young ones as pups, and a group of seals can be called a herd, but a breeding group is a rookery, perhaps because they can be rather vocal like a gathering of rooks?

UK seals

Twenty miles west of mainland Pembrokeshire is a group of rocks called The Smalls and on which stands a lighthouse. The turbulent waters that surround the rocks are teaming with grey seals. On a glorious day in July we set off from the Pembrokeshire mainland aboard a dive boat headed west for the islands. We arrived after a two-hour boat ride to swell surging over the rocks and a fair tide running all around. My husband Tom and I were the only free divers among a boat of scuba divers and with less equipment we were ready first. Shuffling to the back of the rolling boat we slipped into the water close to the rocks. Initially it seemed a little hectic with bubbles from breaking waves fizzing all around us, and the dark shapes of seals zipping by. Once we settled into the conditions, though, we could take a deep breath and sink down to the deeper tranquillity of the kelp. The seals seemed most relaxed here and would come and lie with us staring deep into our eyes or nibbling at our fins, an experience that will remain with us for a long time.

Grey seal.

The two species of seal that inhabit UK coastal waters are Atlantic grey seal *Halichoerus grypus* which translates as 'sea-pig with a hooked-nose' and harbour or common seal, *Phoca vitulina* from the Latin 'plump calf'. Both are charismatic and easily seen from many vantage points along the UK coast. Their distribution around the coast reflects their breeding site preferences. Grey seals favour uninhabited islands, secluded beaches and sea caves, while harbour seals prefer either sheltered rocky shores or sandy estuaries. The UK hosts 40 percent of the world population of grey seals which are spread along the SW coast of England, Wales, West and North Scotland, including Orkney and Shetland, and selected spots along the east coast of Scotland, England and Ireland. Harbour seals, often referred to as common seals, are less abundant in the UK than the grey seals. The islands and indented coastlines of Scotland and Ireland provide ideal conditions on rocky shores, while the big sandy estuaries of the whole UK coast support large numbers on their intertidal banks. The Wash, on the east coast of England, is the single biggest stronghold for harbour seals in the UK and probably the world, being frequented by more than six thousand seals. They are absent from the south and south-west coast of England and Wales.

Breeding

Both seals have well-defined periods of pupping and mating through the year that differ from each other. Males of neither species take any part in rearing pups; the females take sole responsibility for a brief but intense period of parental care. Single pups are born and fed with fat rich milk. In both species, the females become fertile immediately after pupping so mating occurs directly after the pups are weaned.

Grey seal

The pupping season for grey seals is roughly in the autumn months, but it gets progressively later as you move around the UK from north

The grey seal cow gives birth to her pup on secluded storm beaches.

to south in a clockwise direction. The first pups are born in Cornwall and South Wales in August and September compared with November to December in Scotland and down the east coast of England.

Female grey seals come ashore on secluded beaches and sea caves to give birth and rear their pups. Each gives birth to single pup with a thick, white coat that provides insulation while on the land. They are attentive parents, spending several weeks feeding their pups and losing up to 65kg in the process. The pups drink two and a half litres of milk every day, which is made up of 60 percent fat; it is so rich that pups can grow by as much as 30kg in two weeks, tripling their birth weight. They do not grow much in length during this time but increase in girth, piling on the blubber that will act as both insulation and food store in the weeks to come. After around three weeks, females leave their pups and head back out to sea where they feed for the first time since

The new born grey seal pup is thin with loose folds of skin (top) that soon fill out on the fat-rich milk delivered by their attentive mothers (bottom).

giving birth. They also become fertile shortly after pupping, so will mate again. The pups can spend up to two weeks alone on the beach while they summon the courage to take to the sea and learn to fish for themselves. They will also moult the white coat of birth, revealing their sleek fur of adulthood.

Male grey seals are distinguished from females by their thick neck, Roman nose profile and confident air. They appear when the first pups are born and compete with each other for a position in the breeding group. Males attempt to exclude other males from a particular group of females and may have between two and ten females that he mates with. He will guard those females from other males, patrolling both the beach and nearby waters vigilantly. While the females are lactating, they will not entertain the males and are often seen fending off their amorous advances. Once the pups are weaned mating can take place either on the beach or in the water where it may be accompanied by energetic bouts of rolling and flipper splashing. At the end of the mating season males and females go their separate ways until the following season.

Grey bull seals have thick, folded necks, a Roman-style nose and are large (top) while the females have a more dog-like head profile and speckled fur (bottom).

Harbour seal

Females give birth to a single pup in June or July each year. Pups are very well developed at birth and can swim and dive within a few hours; for this reason they lack the white coat of other species of pups. This enables common seals to breed in estuaries where sandbanks are exposed for only part of the day. Mothers feed their young with an extremely rich milk and pups grow rapidly, doubling their birth weight during the three or four weeks that they suckle. As with grey seals, mating occurs as soon as the pups are weaned.

Moulting

Once a year, both seal species undergo moulting, whereby the outer layer of hair and skin is shed to maintain its condition. This process takes up to a month to complete, during which time they will haul out on the land and do not feed. Studies have shown that when moulting, the seals' skin temperature becomes very warm as blood is circulated close to the skin surface to allow rapid hair growth. This requires spending a lot of energy during the moult. To avoid losing heat, the seals increase the time spent ashore, and spend less time in the cold water where they would become chilled.

The moulting of grey seals is delayed for three to five months after mating, occurring between January and March according to where they live in the UK. With harbour seals the moult follows close behind, breeding from mid-July to early September.

Feast and fast

Feeding is dictated by the seals' breeding and moulting cycles. Females do not feed while pupping, focusing all their efforts on providing for the pup. Males similarly cannot afford the distraction of fishing while patrolling their hard-won females, and they too live off their fat reserves during breeding season. Another period of fasting occurs during the moult. At other times of the year the diet of grey and harbour seals includes a variety of fish species, particularly those that live on or near the seabed. Cod, flatfish, herring, skates and sand eels are all on the menu and they may be pursued in vigorous chases. While on a boat on the south side of Skomer a few years ago I remember watching a grey seal chase a fish through the water; the fish leapt clear of the surface three times with the seal in hot pursuit before eventually winning the race.

Aside from fish, seals will eat whatever is available including crabs, lobsters, shrimps and octopus. More recent observations and studies from Scotland, the Netherlands, Germany and Pembrokeshire show that grey seals will also prey and feed on harbour porpoises.

I witnessed this for myself in Ramsey Sound, Pembrokeshire July 2015. I was watching the sea for porpoise activity and from a distance saw a commotion of gulls bobbing and dipping at the water surface. I lifted my binoculars to get a better look and was puzzled to see the tail of a porpoise rising vertically out of the water, brandished by a seal. The gore of the scene hit me as the seal tore into the spongy blubber, creating an expanding pool of blood across the water surface. Over the next few minutes the seal enjoyed the feast then quickly sank from view with its prize, leaving no trace of what had just happened.

Seal senses

Seals certainly use all their senses while hunting underwater and both their sight and hearing are excellent. Vision underwater is enhanced with enlarged, rounded lenses adapted to underwater light conditions. The eyes also contain high numbers of photoreceptor cells called rod cells; these are sensitive to low light levels and well-developed tapetum lucidum, a layer of reflecting plates behind the retina. These plates act as mirrors to reflect light back through the retina, further enhancing their low-light vision. Underwater the pupils dilate into a

The large, round eyes enhance vision underwater while the highly sensitive whiskers locate fish with precision.

Diving specialists

Like us, seals breathe air and when they dive underwater must do so on a single breath of air. The mammalian diving response is a remarkable behaviour that overrides their basic reflexes in order to conserve limited oxygen stores. It is most studied in large aquatic mammals but is seen in all vertebrates, including diving birds (as mentioned in the *Seabirds* chapter) but also all land birds and mammals including humans. The response is triggered by immersing the face in cool water and produces unconscious, reflexive changes that include cessation of breathing (apnea), a reduction in heart rate (bradycardia) and narrowing of blood vessels to divert blood from the extremities to the vital organs (peripheral vasoconstriction). These responses are completely reflexive and happen the moment the face and nostrils hit the water. If you're not quite convinced that this includes you and you have a heart rate monitor handy try this home experiment. Put your heart monitor on and notice your resting heart rate. Assuming you are quite happy having your face in water and holding your breath, run a sink full of cold water, take a breath and plunge your face in. You may need a helper at this stage to watch the

wide circle to let in as much light as possible; if you've been lucky enough to swim with a seal you will have noticed the striking, round eyes. Seals also hear very well in both water and air. Underwater they may use hearing to detect the sound of potential prey from afar then home in using their other senses. Hearing is probably more important for communication with other seals; females and pups often call to each other and adults may growl and grunt underwater, especially during the breeding season.

The coarse, prominent whiskers provide their main sense when it comes to feeding. Seals have super-sensitive whiskers and studies have shown that without sight or hearing the whiskers alone can accurately pinpoint fish several metres away. As they are swept from side to side the whiskers pick up on vibrations created by the prey, allowing them to detect movements hidden from sight.

heart rate monitor, but what you'll notice is that your heart rate drops quite quickly and will drop significantly if you have a good breath hold. In fact, this is a great way to calm yourself if you are feeling anxious but, please exercise caution and come up for air when you feel the need.

Breath-holding masters

Studies have shown that the mammalian heart rate slows by approximately 10–25 percent soon after immersion and becomes slower on long dives; this reduces the rate of oxygen entering the bloodstream, allowing the body to retain it for use by the vital organs. Accompanying this is the constriction of blood capillaries in the extremities so that oxygenated blood gets shunted toward the heart, lungs, brain and other vital organs. For seals, physiological adaptations also enhance the diving lifestyle. Myoglobin is an oxygen-binding protein found in muscle tissue and is especially abundant in diving mammals, reaching 10–30 times that of land animals. True seals store two thirds of their oxygen in blood haemoglobin, just under a third in muscle myoglobin, and the rest in the lungs. As seals dive deeper contraction of the spleen is triggered as part of

Grey seals can hold their breath for more than an hour.

the diving response. The spleen is large in seals and capable of storing inordinate amounts of red blood cells in diving mammals, so when it contracts a fresh supply of haemoglobin-rich blood is delivered to the circulatory system. The mammalian dive reflex is an evolutionary adaptation essential to being able to remain underwater for extended periods of time which

seals take full advantage of. Dive times of more than an hour have been reported for grey seals and twenty-five minutes for harbour seals; certainly enviable statistics for a freediving photographer like myself. For seals, though, it's more about maximising time in pursuit of a meal. Their depth skills are also impressive; grey seals are known to dive to a depth of

300 metres and regularly forage for fish at 70 metres. Elephant seals top both the longest breath-hold and deepest dive stakes though, with a breath hold time of 100 minutes and depth of 2,388 metres.

Staying warm

Life in cold water is a challenge for a warm-blooded mammal. Water conducts heat thirteen times faster than air so conserving body heat requires some modifications from those choosing to call it home. Body surface in contact with the water will lose heat. When I'm in the water for any length of time I dress myself in a thick layer of insulating neoprene in the form of a wetsuit. Seals have evolved two ways of minimising heat loss. First they insulate themselves with blubber, a thick layer of fat just under the skin that may be up to ten centimetres thick in seals living in freezing polar waters. Fur also provides insulation, and some are more furry than others; fur seals have very dense fur coats and not so much blubber.

The second key to maintaining body heat is a body surface area that is much reduced compared to the volume. The larger they are, the smaller the surface area compared to volume and hence heat loss potential. This may explain why the smallest seal is the tropical dwelling Galápagos fur seal *Arctocephalus galapagoensis* (female 35 kg) and the largest is the southern elephant seal *Mirounga leonina* (male 4,000 kg) that inhabitants the icy South Pole. Shape is also important but there must be a compromise between streamlining and heat conservation; while a sphere is the best shape for staying warm, the middle ground is a rotund torpedo that achieves the best of both worlds.

Dr Lou's low-down ... Suspended development

Seals are among a hundred or so different animals that delay the development of their fertilised egg after mating. During a three to four-month period, growth of the fertilised egg is suspended while held in the uterus, after which a hormonal change triggers continued development. With their nine-month gestation period, this ensures that pupping occurs at the same time each year. For an animal that spends most of the year spread throughout the ocean, this strategy means they can both pup and mate in the same few party months.

Short-beaked common dolphin bow-riding off the Pembrokeshire coast, Wales.
Photo credit: Lyndon Lomax.

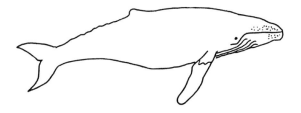

Cetaceans

Whales, dolphins and porpoises make up the highly specialised group of aquatic mammals known as cetaceans. There are around ninety species worldwide that include the largest animal that has ever lived, the blue whale, the highly intelligent and communicative dolphins, tusked narwhals, blind river dolphins and singing humpback whales. The group is divided into two categories – baleen whales and toothed whales. Baleen plates, or whalebone, are comb-like bristles that hang from the upper jaw of the large baleen whales and allow them to filter-feed. When these whales open their mouths, water and prey, such as krill or small fish upon which they feed, pour in. The water floods back out but the baleen filters out the prey for the whale to swallow. Blue, humpback, grey and right whales are all included in this group.

The vast majority of whales and dolphins, however, belong in the toothed category, and they feed on prey in a similar manner to most carnivores. These include the beaked whales, the dolphins and the porpoises. The sperm whale is the only large whale in this category and is well-equipped with teeth, as are the killer whale, beluga and narwhal. There are many places around the UK coast to view cetaceans; twelve species can be regularly seen in UK waters:

1. Harbour porpoise, *Phocoena phocoena*
2. Short-beaked common dolphin, *Delphinus delphis*
3. Bottlenose dolphin, *Tursiops truncatus*
4. White-beaked dolphin, *Lagenorhynchus albirostris*
5. Atlantic white-sided dolphin, *Lagenorhynchus acutus*
6. Risso's dolphin, *Grampus griseus*
7. Killer whale, *Orcinus orca*
8. *Long-finned pilot whale, Globicephalus melas*
9. Humpback whale, *Megaptera novaeangliae*
10. Minke whale, *Balaenoptera acutorostrata*
11. Fin whale, *Balaenoptera physalus*
12. Sperm whale, *Physeter macrocephalus*

Many are seen frequently and are considered resident at numerous locations throughout the year, while others put in fleeting appearances during the summer months while on migration. Humpbacks have been visiting UK waters more and more since 2004; in 2013 a humpback was seen off the Norfolk coast for the first time since written records began for the area – and there is evidence that some of them may be returning individuals. They pass each year as part of their migration between feeding grounds in the North Atlantic and breeding grounds in the Caribbean and Azores. Experts think the rise in UK sightings could be linked to a general increase in their population sizes, which have been recovering globally since commercial whaling bans last century. Quite the opposite to humpback whales, harbour porpoises are the most common and widespread of UK cetaceans and seen in many locations throughout the year.

More than half of the species listed above can be viewed from the coast, while the others require you to get on a boat and travel a few miles offshore to be in with a chance. As the scope of this guide is coastal and not offshore, I believe there are six candidates you are most likely to see from a good vantage point on the land, or while exploring along the coast in a small craft. In descending order of potential sighting: harbour porpoise, bottlenose dolphin, common dolphin, Risso's dolphin, minke whale, killer whale. Your location in the UK will certainly influence your chances, as there are hotspots for certain species. I happen to know that if you were to visit the south end of Ramsey Sound near St David's in Pembrokeshire in calm weather on an ebbing tide, with a keen eye and a pair of binoculars you would be highly likely to see harbour porpoise but not bottlenose dolphins. Head to Cardigan Bay in the neighbouring county on the other hand and your chances of seeing the resident bottlenose dolphins would rate high. In Scotland, the Hebridean Whale Trail was launched by the Hebridean Whale and Dolphin Trust in summer 2019. Over 30 shore-based sites from the Clyde to Cape Wrath and out to

St Kilda are included in the trail with guidance on the best locations to spot particular species of cetaceans, www.whaletrail.org.

I have focused this chapter on a few species that I have been lucky enough to encounter while exploring near to shore.

Harbour porpoise

A few years ago, I spent several months watching the sea from tidal headlands in the Ramsey sound area; I was working on a contract for an energy company trialling a tidal turbine that needed to monitor marine wildlife activity in the area. For many hours I would be alert for signs of harbour porpoise and other marine mammals passing. Porpoise are pretty much resident on this particular stretch of coast so they made up most of my observations, with regular grey seal sightings too and the occasional pod of Risso's dolphins thrown in for excitement. I would often wonder about the life of porpoises in my peaceful hours of observing them from afar; what did they do from day to day in the murky waters? What exactly did they eat for their last meal and where did they go at night?

The harbour porpoise is very much a coastal cetacean, feeding in the fast-flowing waters of tidal headlands.

Being coastal in its habits the harbour porpoise, *Phocoena phocoena*, is the UK's most familiar cetacean and one you are most likely to see from a sea kayak or while walking the coastal path. It is the smallest member of the Odontocetes, the tooth-bearing dolphins, with adults measuring up to two metres in length and weighing up to 70 kilograms. Their short beak and small, rather portly physique topped with a dark triangular dorsal fin make them easy to distinguish from other species.

Combine these features with their generally mild behaviour and the way they roll from beak to tail fluke when surfacing for air, and their identity becomes unmistakable. In common with many other cetaceans, female porpoises are larger than males due to the greater energy demands of pregnancy and lactation. Single calves are born in spring and are cared for by their mothers for up to two years. Initially they are sustained by their mother's fat-rich milk, but they soon learn to catch fish.

Puffing pigs

The English word porpoise comes from the French pourpois, which is from Medieval Latin porcopiscus, a compound of porcus (pig) and piscus (fish). In Danish it is marsvin and Dutch mereswijn, sea swine. Fishermen in New England and eastern Canada also call them puffers or puffing pigs, a fitting description you will realise when one surfaces close-by. Their global population of 700,000 or so prevails in the cooler waters of the northern hemisphere with a discontinuous distribution from West Greenland to Cape Hatteras, and from the Barents Sea to West Africa. In the North Pacific, they are found from Japan north to the Chukchi Sea and from Monterey Bay to the Beaufort Sea.

Ultrasonic hearing

In *Dr Lou's low-down* on page 40, I explained how light is attenuated as it travels to the depths in coastal waters. The resulting deterioration of light impairs the vision of animals living there. For porpoise and their fellow toothed whales, hearing is the primary sense due to sound being transmitted far better than light underwater. Millions of years of evolution have modified the ear structure and honed special organs to aid echolocation

and communication with other porpoises. By contracting air sacs in the nasal passages, they produce high-powered clicks that are focused and directed by a mass of tissue in the forehead called the melon. The echoes reflected back at their ears are then used to create a detailed sound picture, enabling them to go about their business in complete darkness or murky water.

The sounds emanating from an echolocating porpoise are extremely high frequency and well beyond perception by the human ear. Such ultrasonic sound is highly beneficial for micro-navigation and accurate location of prey but is only audible at close quarters; studies have estimated that in order to hear one another porpoise must remain within a one-kilometre range. This contrasts with some of the larger whale species, such as the humpback whale, whose low frequency vocalisations travel thousands of miles through oceans to be heard by whales on the other side of the planet.

Porpoise spend a large percentage of their time foraging so they need to frequent prey-rich waters. The strong tidal currents that funnel through sounds and squeeze around headlands bring a plentiful supply of food for the porpoise and they hunt by facing into the tide to catch

fish as they are brought to them in the flow. Each fish is swallowed whole allowing several fish to be caught in quick succession and lined up in the gullet like a string of sausages.

Several years ago, on a calm summer's evening, I headed out to one of the tidal headlands in my sea kayak to marvel at the river of Manx shearwaters heading back to Skomer island for nightfall. Drifting gently among the endless flow of gliding birds, a strange noise startled me. "Pffffrt-pfff," followed by the smooth back and understated rise of a harbour porpoise as it surfaced for air. I stop breathing for a second or two, the breath catching in my chest at this surprise visit from Europe's smallest cetacean. I'd seen a lot of porpoises over the years, from the land, through binoculars, mainly at a distance, but this was different. Being close enough to hear the breath, the renewal of air into the lungs, made me realise our connection through that breath. The harbour porpoise may not be the most flamboyant of dolphins, but it's still thrilling to behold this tiny puffing pig.

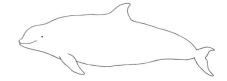

Minke whale

Catching sight of a whale for the first time is an unforgettable experience and especially so from the water in a kayak or while swimming. Excitement and awe flood your being and mingle with a less tangible emotion, one of deep connection, love you might say. I felt it when I saw my first whale, a minke fishing in the tide off the tidal headland of Rubha Hunish on the north tip of Skye. Our guide book, Scottish Sea Kayaking: fifty great sea kayak voyages by Doug Cooper and George Reid, listed this stretch of coast among the classic trips of Scotland and suggested "... you may be lucky enough to see a Minke whale." Tom saw it first, a dark expanse followed by a fin that scythed through the water surface. It moved swiftly and sank before I could turn in my seat to see it. As I waited for it to rise again, scanning this way and that, my heart pounded in my ears. With a burst of exhaled air it surfaced not far away; my skin prickled with excitement and I let out a little squeal. I had just learned to Eskimo roll and I wondered if I might need to perform my first roll in anger as a result of being toppled by a surfacing whale.

Minke whale at Rubha Hunish, Isle of Skye, Scotland.

It appeared to be doing laps in the tide, drifting for a time then swimming back against the flow to reposition near the headland where the flow was greatest. We followed suit for a few rounds then gave thanks to the whale and allowed ourselves to get pushed east.

Furrow-throated filter feeders

The minke whale is the smallest of all large whales, a group called the rorquals that includes the blue whale. The word rorqual comes from the Norwegian word *rorhval* which means furrow and refers to the many throat grooves that extend from underneath the lower jaw to behind the flippers in all members of the group. The grooves allow huge expansion of the mouth cavity when they are feeding, allowing them to take in tonnes of water and filter out the fish or krill with their baleen. Though the minke whale is the smallest member of the rorquals it can grow to ten metres long; it is also the most abundant of the large whales and occurs virtually worldwide in tropical, temperate and polar waters of both hemispheres. They are seen in UK waters between April and October on migration between feeding and breeding grounds. The best place to see them is the coastal and inshore waters around the Hebrides in Scotland. Here they are generally solitary but can sometimes be seen feeding in groups of up to ten, engulfing huge mouthfuls of sand eels, herring and whiting.

Risso's dolphin

My first sighting of Risso's dolphins was from the cliff top at St David's Head in Pembrokeshire. Seven scything fins sliced through the water, bright white and luminous in the morning sunlight. These large, distinctive dolphins were travelling fast in a tight group, breaching so that I got to see the pale expanse of them in the air. They flowed quickly past, hurried on by the tide and though about a kilometre from my cliff-top stance, their energy was infectious. I have since felt their energy through sightings that friends have had while sea kayaking off the north coast of Anglesey, when a pod passed right beneath their boats.

These are large, boisterous dolphins that, although described as offshore in their habits, have been sighted regularly at coastal locations in recent years; year-round sightings have been reported for Anglesey and Strumble Head, Pembrokeshire over the last few years. The best places to spot Risso's Dolphins in the UK are Cornwall, South West and North West Wales, North East Scotland and North West Ireland.

Risso's dolphin. Photo credit: Lyndon Lomax.

Squid wrestlers

Risso's dolphins are relatively easy to identify at sea. They have a robust, stocky body and a tall, sickle shaped dorsal fin; the forehead is blunt and bulbous. The colour varies from white to dark grey and as they age, their body becomes scratched and scarred from the teeth of other Risso's dolphins and prey species such as squid. Unusually for toothed whales, Risso's dolphins have no teeth in the upper jaw and between only two and seven pairs in the lower. Their teeth are merely used to grip their soft prey of squid and octopus which are swallowed whole. They are able to dive for up to thirty minutes down to depths of 400–500 metres, and sometimes forage cooperatively.

Adult Risso's dolphins may be almost four metres in length and can live for more than thirty years. From a distance their large size and tall dorsal fin often causes momentary confusion with small killer whales or bottlenose dolphins. They are sociable, travelling in groups of three to fifty individuals, and may sometimes be seen in mixed schools travelling with other species of dolphin. They are distributed throughout the deep tropical and warm temperate waters in both northern and southern hemispheres.

Bottlenose dolphin

As their name suggests bottlenose dolphins have a short thick beak, a curved mouth that gives them a permanent smile and a large, sickle-shaped dorsal fin that is often marked with notches and scratches. They are grey in colour with a robust body and head, measuring two to four metres in length and weighing in anywhere between 150–650kg. They are highly sociable and travel in groups called pods of around 10–15 dolphins that hunt together, as well as cooperate to raise young dolphin calves. Members of the group communicate with each

Bottlenose dolphins often breach clear of the water (above) and are lively and boisterous (right). Photo credit: Lyndon Lomax.

other by a complex system of squeaks and whistles and also use body language, leaping out of the water, snapping their jaws and even butting heads; displays can be highly boisterous with plenty of breaching and splashing. Each bottlenose dolphin has its own name that comprises a unique set of whistles; this is used by other members of the group to refer to or attract the attention of a particular individual. Like other toothed dolphins they track their fish prey using echolocation and may work as a team to round up fish. In some areas of the world they have been observed chasing fish out of the water, beaching themselves in the process, before wriggling back to the water. Bold behaviour indeed.

Tool-using spongers
Bottlenose dolphins are well-known for their exceptional learning capabilities in captivity and have complex social structures within their pods. In western Australia they have been observed using tools to help them hunt. Certain individuals will break off conical marine sponges from the seabed and wear them over their noses like a glove. It is thought the sponge provides protection for their sensitive snouts as they forage for fish on the seafloor. Researchers discovered that it was mainly females that took up 'sponging' and that this skill was passed on to their offspring and represents the first example of tool use being passed on culturally in a marine mammal.

Dolphin friend
Though mostly found in small groups, some individuals, usually males, do live solitary lives and may seek out swimmers and small boats, remaining in the same area for years. The Dingle dolphin – also known as Fungie – is a wild, male bottlenose dolphin that has been interacting with swimmers and boats off the Dingle coast in Ireland for many years. According to locals he was first seen in the harbour in 1983 and continues to seek out human contact over thirty years later. Bottlenose dolphins are widely distributed in cold temperate to tropical seas worldwide. They are found all around the UK but best places to see them are Moray Firth in Scotland, Cardigan bay in Wales and off Cornwall.

Short-beaked common dolphin

Having booked an evening boat trip to circumnavigate Ramsey Island with our friends and watch Manx shearwaters return from a day of fishing, the sea conditions were too lumpy to head out west. Instead we opted to enjoy the company of seals on the sheltered east side of the island. Drifting near the bachelor beach heaped up with seals lounging above the tide line, our skipper suddenly noticed a commotion at the far south end of Ramsey Sound. Gannets circled above the spot where harbour porpoise are often spotted fishing in the tide but we soon realised it was a lively pod of common dolphins, including several calves, swimming in unison with their mums. As we neared the group, they headed our way and started to bow ride the boat, rising at speed to show us their glistening backs, occasionally leaping clear of the water in a dynamic display of apparent joy. Everyone aboard was instantly charged with excitement and buzzed from the dolphins spirited energy. The realisation that a group of wild creatures was aware of us and wanted to interact was universally exciting and humbling, and touched us all.

Dolphins aplenty

Short-beaked common dolphins are one of the smaller species of dolphin, growing to around 2.5m and a maximum weight of 200kg. Their colouration is tricoloured, grey, white and tan or yellow in a distinctive hourglass pattern along the side. They are characteristically fast, energetic swimmers, jumping and splashing with several group members often surfacing together. These lively dolphins form pods of 10–30 animals which may then group together to form super- or megapods with thousands of individuals. They are one of the most abundant cetaceans with estimates in the several hundred thousands worldwide. As with other social dolphins they are highly vocal; their high-pitched communication whistles can often be heard above the surface when they are bow riding the boat. Although considered an offshore species they often come close to shore to feed on squid and small schooling fish and will work together to herd fish into tight balls. Like many other dolphin species, the common dolphin will sometimes take advantage of commercial fishing activities, feeding on fish escaping from the nets or discarded

The joy of seeing dolphins is hard to put in to words; common dolphin off the coast of Pembrokeshire, Wales.

by the fishermen. Despite being abundant, their attraction to fishing nets is a fatal one with many getting trapped inside. This has contributed to an overall decline in numbers in recent years. Globally, short-beaked common dolphins inhabit tropical and warm temperate seas and can be found in both coastal and offshore waters. They are found all around the UK and are most common off south and west coasts and offshore.

Dr Lou's low-down ... Trophic cascades

One of the most exciting scientific findings of the last fifty years is the discovery of trophic cascades. The term derives from how ecologists group animals and plants in an ecosystem according to how they feed; each group is assigned a trophic level (the word trophic means food or feeding) so that a food chain develops with predators at the top and herbivores and plants below. Changing the number of animals at the top trophic level can have an effect that cascades down through all trophic levels, impacting every animal and plant that forms a link in the chain.

Research on whales has revealed them to be key predators in the oceans that trigger a classic example of trophic cascade when they become scarce. Whales eat fish and krill so you might expect that killing whales would boost the numbers of fish and krill and therefore the food available for other fishers to eat. But as commercial whaling efforts peaked in the early twentieth century and the number of great whales declined, so did the numbers of fish and

krill. But how can it be that removing a predator causes the numbers of their prey to decrease and not increase as logic would predict? We now know this to be due to the cascading effect caused by removing a key predator from a finely balanced ocean system; scientists have worked out that not only do whales help to keep their prey alive but they help to sustain the entire living system. And it all comes down to two movements, swimming and defecation.

Whales often dive to great depths to feed and as they return, they release vast clouds of poo called faecal plumes that are very rich in iron and nitrogen. In fact, scientists working in the Southern Ocean found iron concentrations in whale poo to be 10 million times that of the surrounding Antarctic seawater. All this extra iron and nitrogen serves to fertilise the plant plankton that thrive in the light saturated surface waters of the photic zone, where nutrients are scarce. Productivity is further enhanced by the vertical movements of the

whales up and down through the water column which has a mixing effect, returning nutrients and plant plankton back to the surface. It has been estimated that the vertical mixing of water caused by the movement of animals up and down through the oceans is roughly the same as the amount of mixing caused by all the world's wind, waves and tides. It is an astonishing realisation that many of the ocean's larger inhabitants act as ecosystem engineers whose presence help to maintain the health and stability of the world's oceans.

This means that where there is more plant plankton there is more animal plankton on which the larger creatures feed and more whales means more fish and krill. But the story does not end there; the plant plankton also absorbs carbon dioxide from the atmosphere. When it eventually dies and sinks to the deep ocean it takes this carbon out of circulation down to a place where it remains for thousands of years. More whales equal more plankton which equal more carbon absorption. In their historical heyday, before commercial whaling decimated their numbers, they may have been responsible for removing tens of millions of tonnes of carbon from the atmosphere every year. In a nutshell, whales change the climate.

Until recently large creatures occupying the top trophic level were plentiful and widespread across the globe and had been for millions of years. The loss of these animals may be humankind's most pervasive influence on the natural world. Yet science has shown that allowing the great whales to recover could reverse some of the damage we have wrought by increasing the productivity of plant plankton. Their role in the functioning of our planet may be vital and we may need to save the whales in order to save ourselves. As observed by the great naturalist John Muir "When we try to pick out anything by itself, we find it hitched to everything else in the Universe." We are as connected to whales as they are to plankton ...

From plankton to whales, seaweeds to fishes and the very air we breathe, everything is connected.

On open water give rafting seabirds space.

Exploring Lightly: Mindful Curiosity

Mindfulness: "the quality or state of being conscious or aware of something"

Being mindful in our daily lives is something every one of us can benefit from and certainly a quality we will all have practised during quiet moments in nature. Picture a moment when you have been fully absorbed in a joyful activity, your mind is focused on each movement of your body, the sound of the wind across your ears, birds calling overhead and the sensation of your breath rising and falling in your chest, like waves swishing up and down the shore. This kind of mindful attention can be applied to our exploration of the ocean and coastal environment so that our experiences are harmonious for ourselves and the planet. When exploring wildlife rich areas there is often potential to have a negative effect. Through awareness of our own conduct on the water and along the coast in relation to our surroundings we can act to minimise detrimental impacts. Witnessing the buzz and clamour of a seabird colony, cruising along coasts popular with breeding seals or being startled by a porpoise as it burst to the surface for breath are all truly memorable experiences. To support such experiences best practice guidelines for marine wildlife watching and voluntary codes of conduct have been developed in many areas of the UK and beyond. Though heavily focused on boat-based cetacean watching in response to a boom in whale and dolphin tourism worldwide, seals, seabirds, basking sharks and otters have also been considered in detail in certain areas.

Fast moving, noisy power boats pose an obvious threat to marine animals swimming at the surface, while exploring by kayak, paddle board or swimming would appear benign in comparison. Unlike a boat with an engine, paddle craft and swimmers tend not to announce their presence with noise. We can creep along and turn a corner silently, innocently startling wildlife and causing a surprising amount of disturbance. In some places seals and seabirds have become habituated to regular traffic created by wildlife tour boats and these boats can approach colonies with little effect on the animal's behaviour. Visit the very same colonies in a sea kayak and the members get fidgety before you get even half as close. I write from personal experience at particular locations, Ramsey Island in Pembrokeshire being an example, but this certainly varies from place to place. A sea kayaker's ability to reach and land at places other boats cannot, means we may end up unsettling wildlife causing undue stress and disturbance to their day.

Guillemots breed on narrow ledges where their eggs are easily dislodged if disturbed.

What is disturbance?

"The result of direct or indirect interaction with people that changes the behaviour of an animal or changes the environment, which in turn affects the well-being or survival of an animal in the short, medium or long term."

Many marine species are protected by EU and UK wildlife legislation under the Wildlife and Countryside Act 1981, from intentional or deliberate disturbance. Being alert for behaviour that indicates disturbance will allow you to act in the best interest of the wildlife and enjoy an experience that is harmonious for all concerned. A group of guillemots lined up on a nesting ledge bobbing and craning their heads while flapping their wings, for example, are signs that you may have drifted too close and need to back off.

Why does it matter?

Substantial evidence shows that disturbance can have serious long-term impacts on populations of marine animals. During the breeding season, it may mean a missed feed vital for a seal pup's survival, while disturbing nesting seabirds may send eggs or chicks tumbling over the cliff edge as the adults take to the air in fright. Guillemots are particularly vulnerable as they lay a single egg directly onto the rock ledge and won't lay again that season if the egg is lost. At other times of the year, disturbance may simply create more stress for animals facing increasing modern pressures on their environment.

Codes of Conduct

A plethora of codes has been developed worldwide, aimed specifically at managing wildlife watching. Each gives comprehensive guidelines for specific areas or groups of animals, but the general message and desired outcome is the same; to minimise disturbance to wildlife. When planning a trip be sure to research whether there are areas on your route that are particularly sensitive for wildlife and whether there are specific marine codes of conduct and seasonal access restrictions in place.

The Pembrokeshire Marine Code is an excellent example relevant to all water-based activities including power boating, sailing, sea kayaking, SUP, coasteering and wild swimming in the UK and is outlined below.

Pembrokeshire Marine Code

www.pembrokeshiremarinecode.org.uk
The Pembrokeshire Marine Code was developed in 2002 as a voluntary guide to best practice by local operators and other organisations working closely with the Pembrokeshire Coast National Park Authority and the RSPB. It aims to help protect marine wildlife from disturbance by all water users. A Marine Code for Kayaking was developed from this in association with Canoe Wales to specifically address best practice for sea kayakers in Pembrokeshire.

The guidelines include a series of Marine Code maps that detail seasonal access restrictions to particularly sensitive areas of the coast for seabirds and Atlantic grey seals. The restrictions apply from 1st March to 31st July for sea birds nesting on sea cliffs and from 1st August

Outdoor operators in Pembrokeshire run their activities with the Pembrokeshire Marine Code in mind, including coasteering at Abereiddy where grey seal pups are often encountered.

to 30th November for Atlantic grey seal pupping beaches and bays to correspond with their breeding seasons. The maps and a host of other useful resources are available in the Marine Code App which is free to download for both Android and Apple. The app will automatically alert you when you are in the vicinity of a sensitive area and direct you towards the relevant map. Alternatively, the maps can be downloaded directly from the Pembrokeshire Marine Code website and are also available in a waterproof version that fits neatly in your pocket, buoyancy aid or rucksack (contact the Marine Code Officer directly for your copy). The maps are an essential resource to have to hand when planning coastal trips in Pembrokeshire, empowering you to minimise disturbance to the wildlife that makes this area so special. The Pembrokeshire Outdoor Charter Group has also produced an excellent

Pembrokeshire Marine Code map for Ramsey Island showing seasonal access restrictions for seals (pink), sea birds (orange) and both seals and sea birds (yellow).

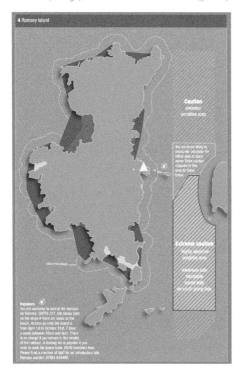

video outlining best practice for sea kayaking the wildlife rich coasts of Wales, *Sea Kayaking in Wales: reconciling conservation and recreation.* It provides a wonderful overview of how to paddle lightly in Welsh waters as well as some great footage of wildlife and will certainly get you inspired for a trip to Wales.

Other UK marine wildlife watching codes

Marine wildlife watching codes specific to other areas of the UK have been developed and are listed below:

Wales

The Gwynedd Marine Code was launched in 2016. It has since been rolled out to other areas of mid and north Wales coasts and has plans to develop the code through mapping as has been developed in Pembrokeshire. It is available via the Gwynedd Council website www.gwynedd.llyw.cymru.

Scotland

The *Scottish Marine Wildlife Watching Code* is available via the Scottish Natural Heritage website www.nature.scot.

England

Although there is no over-arching marine wildlife code of conduct for England, area specific guidelines have been developed by local groups and stakeholder organisations. For example, Cornwall Marine and Coastal Code group have developed guidelines for watching seals, cetaceans, basking sharks, birds and turtles along the Cornish coast and is available via their website http://cornwallmarinelifecode.org.uk.

General guidance for recreational boaters is provided in *The Green Wildlife Guide for Boaters* available from the Royal Yachting Association website www.rya.org.uk. This gives advice on how to get the best experience from wildlife encounters, while minimising the risk of disturbance and keeping participants and their boats safe.

Before visiting any coastal area of England it's worth using your online search engine to check up on wildlife sensitive areas and local wildlife watching guidelines specific to that area. That way you can plan your recreational activities with the best interests of wildlife in mind.

Ireland

As with England there is no over-arching marine wildlife code of conduct for Ireland but there are

Seals are often curious of kayakers (above) and divers (right) creating memorable experiences.

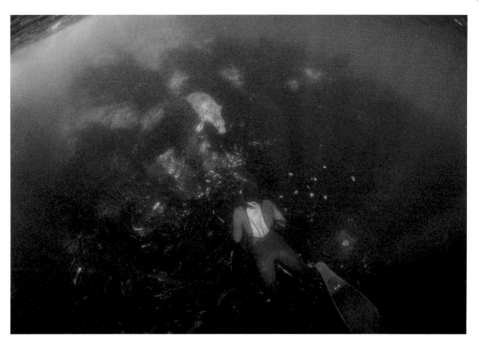

specific guidelines for certain activities and species. Whale watching, for example, is regulated and managed through both national and local guidelines. At a national level, the government has issued *Guidelines for correct procedures when encountering whales and dolphins in Irish coastal waters* (Department of Communications, Marine and Natural Resources Marine Notice No. 15 of 2005) which are designed to inform commercial tour-boat operators and recreational boaters. Additional local guidelines are also operated on a voluntary basis.

I would suggest following general guidelines set out in codes of conduct for other areas of the UK when exploring Ireland.

Marine code top tips summary

- When planning a trip research local marine codes of conduct and observe seasonal access restrictions
- Keep your distance and keep noise to a minimum
- Learn to recognise signs of disturbance for animals you are likely to encounter
- Assess the behaviour of animals from a distance first and approach slowly and quietly from an oblique angle rather than head on or from behind
- During an interaction always allow wildlife to approach you, enjoy the experience then move along

Seashore Code

Exploring the shore at low tide provides fun for all ages and can be enjoyed immeasurably by being mindful of a few simple tips:

- Check the tide times so you know the time of low tide. It's always safest to time your arrival with a dropping tide so you can follow the tide down to low tide. Keep an eye on your watch so you can begin your return before the tide turns and cuts you off.
- Check the weather before you head out so you can be prepared with the right attire to maximise your enjoyment.
- Take only photographs, leaving live animals and plants to continue their life on the shore.
- Treat all living things with respect and replace any stone or seaweed as it was found. Tread carefully when moving over rocks and dipping into rock pools so as not to trample the inhabitants.
- Take part in a beach clean and join the millions of good people worldwide helping to tackle plastic pollution in the marine environment.

#2minutebeachclean

Unfortunately, plastic litter is a common sight on our beaches these days; apart from looking unsightly, plastic pollutes our oceans in a truly insidious way. Through entanglement and ingestion plastic kills marine wildlife; it does not biodegrade but instead breaks down into smaller and smaller pieces becoming microplastics, which adsorb any toxins they come into contact with. These are so small that they float among the plankton that forms the basis of all ocean ecosystems and ends up in the seafood that we eat. One million seabirds and 100,000 marine mammals die each year because of marine litter.

Foraging for seaweeds

Sampling the flavours of the seashore is surely one of summer's culinary delights. Many seaweeds are not only delicious but high in minerals and provide a free and tasty addition to all sorts of dishes. Some are long-lived, while others are seasonal; either way it's good to be mindful of harvesting seaweeds in a sustainable way that allows them to continue growing for months or years to come. Seaweeds show plenty of fresh growth in

During the big storms of 2013 Cornish surfer Martin Dorey was feeling overwhelmed by the scale of the issue so came up with the idea of doing a two-minute beach clean every time he went to the beach and used social media to encourage others to join in. Since its inception in 2013, #2minutebeach-clean has become a global phenomenon with thousands of people taking daily action to reduce plastic litter in the marine environment. Next time you are at the beach spare a quick 2 minutes to pick up some litter and remember to snap a quick photo and share it on social media.

spring and early summer, so this is the most sustainable time of year to sample a few favourites. Due to their strong flavour a small amount provides a delicious garnish; just nip the end from a frond making sure you leave the holdfast (the anchor point) attached to the rock. Only collect what you need for the table and try to sample small amounts from several plants to spread the impact. After a good rinse in fresh water to remove sand and debris, they can be eaten raw or cooked.

Of the 700 or so seaweed species found in UK waters, only two are not recommended as edible; these are found below the low water mark and are mildly acidic, not poisonous. Any seaweed found growing attached to rock between high and low water is therefore a safe bet. Some are tastier than others and those I would recommend are sea lettuce *Ulva lactuca*, sugar kelp *Saccharina latissima*, pepper dulse *Osmundea pinnatifida* and thong weed *Himanthalia elongata*. I would advise introducing them to your diet in moderation, adding them as a garnish to enhance the flavour and nutritional content of your meal, from personal experience too much too soon can have a laxative effect. Happy foraging.

I view my time out along our coasts as a privilege and treat my surroundings with due respect. This includes passing on best practice to fellow explorers when encountering wildlife. Each one of us can be an ambassador for the marine environment by remaining mindful of those we share the oceans with and exploring lightly on our future adventures.

Foraged mindfully, seaweeds are a delicious and highly nutritious addition to many meals.

Dr Lou's low-down ... Ocean optimism

With recent statistics showing catastrophic declines in many habitats and species globally, it is so easy to feel defeated and overwhelmed by the state of our oceans. Climate change, shark finning, whaling, coral reef loss, plastic pollution, overfishing – all stirs feelings of anger, shame and fear that it may be too late to change. Communication about the environment through media channels is sensationally negative, fuelling a culture of hopelessness that threatens to seal the planet's fate. Too often doom-and-gloom stories are the only kind of ocean news we hear, yet evidence from social science suggests that if we do not balance the bad news with good, and the problems with solutions, we will not be motivated to act.

Many good news stories do exist with countless dedicated researchers, organisations and individuals working towards solutions for our oceans. The alternative view is one of understanding, compassion, empathy and hope, powerful emotions rooted in forgiveness. #OceanOptimism began as a Twitter initiative in June 2014 by a group of leading ocean conservationists. They were concerned about the pervasive feelings of despair among the many school children and young scientists they were meeting. Their challenge was to create a social change project that engaged people with ocean conservation successes. #Ocean Optimism has spread widely as a flag for stories reporting progress in marine conservation challenges; since its inception it has reached over 74 million Twitter users.

The Ocean Optimism marine conservation movement focuses on solutions rather than problems, and connections rather than differences, with the aim of creating a new narrative of hope for our oceans. It recognises and respects the many challenges facing our oceans but encourages optimism in order to inspire action. Not long before the publication of this book, Sir David Attenborough stirred up a wave of criticism for his comments during an interview warning against alarmism in TV broadcasts, arguing that talking about drastic environmental problems too often can be counterproductive. Many people disagreed, including environmental journalist George Monbiot who posted a scathing response on Twitter "...by repeatedly failing to show us what is happening, you have betrayed the living world you love so much." I believe there is a middle ground where both the wonders of the natural world are showcased along with the threats and solutions that are working to remedy the problems. Too much disaster language is certainly a "turn-off" (Sir David's words) and overwhelm any rational power to act positively.

It's imperative we all continue to act for the good of our oceans, as humanity cannot survive without them. In the words of Dr Sylvia Earle, oceanographer and explorer, "Even if you never have the chance to see or touch the ocean, the ocean touches you with every breath you take, every drop of water you drink, every bite you consume. Everyone, everywhere is inextricably connected to and utterly dependent upon the existence of the sea."

I urge you to stay optimistic through the doom and gloom of environmental reportage and get behind the swathes of good people working from the heart towards positive solutions. Celebrating the joy propagated by these environmental champions will inspire continued action and a united wave of forward progression. Enjoy the ride!

The glory of encountering barrel jellyfish underwater.

Limpets lined up in a rock niche at low tide.

Bibliography

Seasearch Guide to Seaweeds of Britain and Ireland, Francis Bunker, Christine Maggs, Juliet Brodie, Ann Bunker, Marine Conservation Society 2010, 978-0-948150-51-7

A field key to the British brown seaweeds (Phaeophyta), Field Studies Council 1984

The Biology of Marine Plants, Matthew Dring, Cambridge University Press 1992, 0-521-42765-7

Collins Pocket Guide – Sea Shore of Britain and Europe, Peter Hayward, Tony Nelson-Smith, Chris Shields, Collins 1996, 0002199556

Seashore safaris, Judith Oakley, Graffeg 2010, 1905582331

Rocky Shores, John Archer-Thomson and Julian Cremona, Bloomsbury Wildlife 2019, 978-1-4729-4313-2

Seasearch Guide to Sea Anemones and Corals of Britain and Ireland, Chris Wood, Marine Conservation Society 2005, 0948150416

British anthozoa (Coelenterata: Octocorallia & Hexacorallia), R. Manuel, Academic Press, 1981, 90-04-08596-3

Great British Marine Animals, Paul Naylor, Sound Diving Publications 2011, 978-0-9522831-6-4

Seasearch Guide to Bryozoans and Hydroids of Britain and Ireland, Joanne Porter, Marine Conservation Society 2012, 978-0-948150-56-2

Fishes of the Sea, John and Gillian Lythgoe, Blandford 1991, 0-7137-2225-8

A Field Guide to the Marine Fishes of Wales and Adjacent Waters, Paul Kay, Frances Dipper, Marine Wildlife 2009, 978-0-9562048-0-6

What a Fish Knows, Jonathan Balcombe, Oneworld Publications 2016, 978-1-78607-209-2

Collins Bird Guide, Lars Svenson, Killian Mullarney, Dan Zetterström, Collins 2010, 978-0-00-726814-6

I Am a Poetato, John Hegley, Francis Lincoln Children's Books 2013, 978-1-84780-397-9

Seals (British Natural History Series), Sheila Anderson, Whittet Books Ltd 1990, 0-905483-80-4

Whales, Dolphins and Porpoises, Mark Carwardine, DK Publishing 1995, 0-7513-2781-6

Handbook of Whales, Dolphins and Porpoises, Mark Carwardine, Bloomsbury Wildlife 2019, 978-1472908148

Spying on whales, Nick Pyenson, William Collins 2018, 978-0-00-824450-7

Index